PENGUIN

Troublesome Words

Bill Bryson was born in 1951 in Des Moines, Iowa, and grew up there, but spent most of his adult life in Britain. He worked for *The Times* and was one of the founding journalists on the *Independent*. His books include *Mother Tongue* and *Troublesome Words* (revised edition, 2001), both published by Penguin, and the travel books *The Lost Continent*, *Neither Here Nor There*, *Notes from a Small Island*, *A Walk in the Woods*, *Notes from a Big Country* and *Down Under*. His most recent bestsellers include a biography of Shakespeare, *A Short History of Nearly Everything* and his memoir, *The Life and Times of the Thunderbolt Kid*. He lives in the UK with his wife and four children.

Troublesome Words

BILL BRYSON

PENGUIN BOOKS

PENGUIN BOOKS

Published by the Penguin Group
Penguin Books Ltd, 80 Strand, London WC2R ORL, England
Penguin Group (USA) Inc., 375 Hudson Street, New York, New York 10014, USA
Penguin Group (Canada), 90 Eglinton Avenue East, Suite 700, Toronto, Ontario,
Canada M4P 2Y3 (a division of Pearson Penguin Canada Inc.)
Penguin Ireland, 25 St Stephen's Green, Dublin 2, Ireland (a division of Penguin Books Ltd)
Penguin Group (Australia), 250 Camberwell Road, Camberwell, Victoria 3124, Australia
(a division of Pearson Australia Group Pty Ltd)
Penguin Books India Pvt Ltd, 11 Community Centre, Panchsheel Park, New Delhi – 110 017, India
Penguin Group (NZ), 67 Apollo Drive, Rosedale, North Shore 0632, New Zealand
(a division of Pearson New Zealand Ltd)
Penguin Books (South Africa) (Pty) Ltd, 24 Sturdee Avenue, Rosebank, Johannesburg 2196, South Africa

Penguin Books Ltd, Registered Offices: 80 Strand, London WC2R ORL, England

www.penguin.com

First published as *The Penguin Dictionary of Troublesome Words* 1984
Second edition published 1987
Revised under the current title 1997
Third edition published in Viking 2001
Third edition published in Penguin Books 2002
Reissued in Penguin Books 2009

3

Copyright © Bill Bryson, 1984, 1987, 2001
All rights reserved

The moral right of the author has been asserted

Printed in England by Clays Ltd, St Ives plc

ISBN: 978-0-141-04039-4

www.greenpenguin.co.uk

Penguin Books is committed to a sustainable future
for our business, our readers and our planet.
The book in your hands is made from paper
certified by the Forest Stewardship Council.

Contents

Introduction

When I first put together *The Penguin Dictionary of Troublesome Words*, in 1983, I was a diligent young subeditor on *The Times*, and it was a fundamental part of my job to be sensitive to and particular about points of usage. It was, after all, why they employed me, and I took the responsibility seriously.

So seriously, in fact, that when I realized that there were vast expanses of English usage – linguistic Serengetis – that I was not clear about at all, I wrote to a kindly editor at Penguin Books named Donald McFarlan and impetuously suggested that there was a need for a simple guide to the more confusing or problematic aspects of the language and that I was prepared to undertake it. To my astonishment and gratification, Mr McFarlan sent me a contract and, by way of advance, a sum of money carefully gauged not to cause embarrassment or feelings of overworth. Thus armed, I set about trying to understand this wonderfully disordered thing that is the English language.

As I observed in the first edition, the book that resulted might more accurately, if less convincingly, have been called *A Guide to Everything in English Usage That the Author Wasn't Entirely Clear About Until Quite Recently*. Nearly everything in it arose as the product of questions encountered during the course of daily newspaper work: should it be 'fewer than 10 per cent of voters' or 'less than 10 per cent'? Does someone have 'more money than her' or 'than she'?

The answers to such questions are not always easily found. Seeking the guidance of colleagues is, I discovered, dangerous: raise almost any point of usage with two journalists and you will almost certainly get two confident but entirely contradictory answers. Traditional reference works are often little more helpful because they so frequently contradict one another or are a trifle crotchety or assume from the reader a familiarity with the intricacies of grammar that is – in my case, at any rate – generous. Because of such difficulties, many users of English continue to make usage decisions based on little more than durable superstitions and half-formed understandings. Many, for example, doggedly abjure split infinitives in the conviction that it endows their sentences with superior grammar. (It does not.) Others avoid 'hopefully' as if it were actively infectious and instead write the more cumbrous 'it is hoped' to satisfy an obscure point of syntax that, I suspect, few of them could elucidate. Too often for such people the notion of good English has less to do with expressing ideas clearly than with making words conform to some arbitrary pattern.

But at the same time, anything that helps to bring order to the engaging unruliness that is our language is, almost by definition, a good thing. Just as we all agree that clarity is better served if 'cup' represents a drinking vessel and 'cap' something you put on your head, so too, I think, the world is a fractionally better place if we agree to preserve a distinction between 'its' and 'it's', between 'I lay down the law' and 'I lie down to sleep', between 'imply' and 'infer', 'forego' and 'forgo', 'flout' and 'flaunt', 'anticipate' and 'expect', and countless others. The purpose of this book remains to try to explain such distinctions as succinctly and clearly as I am able.

No one, least of all me, has the right to tell you how to organize your words, and there is scarcely an entry in the pages that follow that you may not wish to disregard sometimes and no doubt a few that you may decide to scorn at all times. If you wish to say 'between you and I' or to use 'fulsome' in the sense of lavish, you are entirely within your rights and can certainly find ample supporting precedents among many distinguished writers. But you may also find it useful to know that such usages are at variance with that eccentric, ever-shifting corpus known as Good English.

Some 60 per cent of the material in the book is new. This is not, alas, because I am now 60 per cent better informed than I was eighteen years ago. In fact, very nearly the reverse. I can't begin to tell you (or at least I prefer not to tell you) how many times while reviewing the original text I found myself thinking: 'Why, I didn't know that. I've been making that mistake for years.' The revisions herein consist largely of elaborations on much that I had forgotten I once knew, and additions concerning matters that have come to my attention since. In an alarmingly real sense, the alternative title now could be *Even More Things in English Usage That the Author Wasn't Entirely Clear About Until Quite Recently.*

As in the earlier editions, most of the entries that follow are illustrated with questionable usages from leading British and American publications, and I should point out that the frequency with which some publications are cited has less to do with the quality of their production than with my own reading habits. I have also not hesitated to cite errors committed by the authorities themselves. It is of course manifestly tactless of me to draw attention to the occasional lapses of those on whom I have so unashamedly relied for guidance. My intention in so doing is not to embarrass or challenge them but simply to show how easily such errors are made, and I trust they will continue to be taken in that light.

It is to those authorities – most especially Philip Howard, Sir Ernest Gowers, the incomparable H. W. Fowler and the late Theodore Bernstein – that I am most indebted. I am also deeply grateful to my wife, Cynthia, for her inexhaustible patience and excellent sandwiches (among rather a lot else); to Donald McFarlan, wherever he may now be; to Tony Lacey of Penguin; to my agent and good friend Carol Heaton; and to Keith Taylor and Donna Poppy for their patient and devoted editing of the original and revised manuscripts. To all of them, thank you.

Bill Bryson, April 2001

A Note on Presentation

To impose a consistent system of presentation in a work of this sort can result in the pages of the book being littered with italics, quotation marks or other typographical devices. Bearing this in mind, I have employed a system that I hope will be easy on the reader's eye as well as easy to follow.

Within each entry, the entry word and any other similarly derived or closely connected words are italicized only when the sense would seem to require it. Other words and phrases – synonyms, antonyms, correct/incorrect alternatives, etc. – are set within quotation marks, but again only when the sense requires it. In both cases, where there is no ambiguity, no typographical device is used to distinguish the word.

A

a, an. Do you say 'a hotel' or 'an hotel'? 'A historian' or 'an historian'? The convention is to use *a* before the aspirated 'h' (a house, a hostage) and *an* before a silent 'h'. *An* is indisputably correct before just four words beginning with 'h': hour, honest, honour and heir. Some British authorities also allow *an* before hotel, historian, heroic and hypothesis, but most prefer *a*.

Errors with the indefinite article become especially common when numbers are involved, as here: 'Cox will contribute 10 percent of the equity needed to build a $80 million cable system' (*Washington Post*). Make it *an*. Similarly, *a* is unnecessary in the following and should be deleted: 'With a 140 second-hand wide-bodied jets on the market, the enthusiasm to buy anything soon evaporated' (*Sunday Times*).

abbreviations, contractions, acronyms. Abbreviation is the general term used to describe any shortened word. Contractions and acronyms are types of abbreviation. A contraction is a word that has been squeezed in the middle, so to speak, but has retained one or more of its opening or closing letters, as with *Mr* for *Mister* and *can't* for *cannot*. An acronym is a word formed from the initial letter or letters of a group of words: *radar* for *ra*dio *d*etecting *a*nd *r*anging, and *NATO* for *N*orth *A*tlantic *T*reaty *O*rganization. Abbreviations that are not pronounced as words (IBM, TUC, ITV) are not acronyms; they are just abbreviations.

Whether to write NATO or Nato is normally a matter of preference or house style. American publications tend to capitalize all the letters of abbreviations, even when they are pronounced as words. In Britain, generally the convention is to capitalize only the initial letter when the abbreviation is pronounced as a word and is reasonably well known. Thus most British publications would write Aids and Nato (but probably not Seato). Confusing the issue is the fondness of commercial enterprises for employing typographical novelty in their titles, giving themselves names such as 3i, EXcell or PricewaterhouseCoopers. Whether to respect these quirks is often a problem. As a rough rule, I would suggest that a company's orthographic eccentricities should be noted, possibly even observed, but never overindulged. Just because a company chooses to put a backward letter into its title or to spell its name in small capitals does not entitle it to become a distraction in print.

For abbreviations of all types, try to avoid an appearance of clutter and intrusiveness. Rather than make repeated reference to 'the IGLCO' or 'NOOSCAM', it is usually better to refer to the abbreviated party as 'the committee', 'the institute' or whatever other word is appropriate.

Finally, a separate source of puzzlement, particularly for those of us who grew up outside Britain and the Commonwealth, is the question of when to put a full stop at the end of an abbreviation – whether, for instance, to write *in* or *in.* for *inch* or *Capt* or *Capt.* for *Captain*. The custom is that when the last letter of the abbreviation is the last letter of the full word – that is, when it is a contraction – no punctuation is added, but when the abbreviation stops in the midst of the full word, a full stop is required. Thus one writes *Dr*, *Mr* and *St* for *Doctor*, *Mister* and *Street* (or *Saint*), but *Prof.*, *in.*, and *Capt.* for *Professor*, *inch* and *Captain*. When such words are made plural, an 's' is normally added to the abbreviation, but the abbreviation remains punctuated as if it were still singular. Thus you would write *2 ins.* for *two inches*, but *2 yds* for *two yards*.

accessible. Not -*able*.

accidentally. Misspelled all too often, as here: 'Moranis's absent-minded professor accidently zaps his kids down to Lilliputian proportions' (*Independent*).

accommodate. One of the most misspelled of all words. Note *-mm-*.

accompanist. Not *-iest*.

acidulous, assiduous. *Acidulous* means tart or acid. *Assiduous* means diligent.

acolyte. Not *-ite*.

acoustics. As a science, the word is singular ('Acoustics was his line of work'). As a collection of properties, it is plural ('The acoustics in the auditorium were not good').

acronyms. See ABBREVIATIONS, CONTRACTIONS, ACRONYMS.

activity. Often a sign of prolixity, as here: 'The warnings followed a week of earthquake activity throughout the region' (*Independent*). Just make it 'a week of earthquakes'.

acute, chronic. These two are sometimes confused, which is a little odd as their meanings are sharply opposed. *Chronic* pertains to lingering conditions, ones that are not easily overcome. *Acute* refers to those that come to a sudden crisis and require immediate attention. People in the Third World may suffer from a chronic shortage of food. In a bad year, their plight may become acute.

AD *anno Domini* (Latin), 'in the year of the Lord'. AD should be written before the year (AD 25) but after the century (fourth century AD), and is usually set in small caps. (See also ANNO DOMINI and BC.)

adage. Even the most careful users of English frequently, but unnecessarily, refer to an 'old adage'. An adage is by definition old.

adapter, adaptor. The first is one who adapts (as in a book for theatrical presentation); the second is the device for making appliances work abroad and so on.

adaptor. See ADAPTER, ADAPTOR.

adjective pile-up. Many journalists, in an otherwise commendable attempt to pack as much information as possible into a confined space, often resort to the practice of piling adjectives in front of the subject, as in this *Times* headline: 'Police rape claim woman in court'. Apart from questions of inelegance, such headlines can be confusing, to say the least. A hurried reader, expecting a normal subject–verb–object construction, could at first conclude that the police have raped a claim-woman in court before the implausibility of that notion makes him go back and read the headline again. No reader should ever be required to retrace his steps, however short the journey. Although the practice is most common in headlines, it sometimes crops up in text, as here: 'His annual salary is accompanied by an up to 30 per cent performance bonus' (*Observer*). The ungainliness there could instantly be obviated by making it 'accompanied by a performance bonus of up to 30 per cent'.

administer. Not *administrate*.

admit to is nearly always wrong, as in these examples: 'The Rev. Jesse Jackson had just admitted to fathering a child with an adoring staffer' (*Baltimore Sun*); 'Pretoria admits to raid against Angola' (*Guardian* headline); 'Botha admits to errors on Machel cash' (*Independent* headline). Delete *to* in each case. You admit a misdeed, you do not admit to it.

advance planning. The *advance* in *advance planning* is always redundant. All planning must be done in advance.

adverse, averse. 'He is not adverse to an occasional brandy' (*Observer*). The word wanted here was *averse*, which means reluctant or disinclined (think of *aversion*). *Adverse* means hostile and antagonistic (think of *adversary*).

aerate. Just two syllables. Not *aereate*.

affect, effect. As a verb, *affect* means to influence ('Smoking may affect your health') or to adopt a pose or manner ('He affected ignorance'). *Effect* as a verb means to accomplish ('The prisoners effected an escape'). As a noun, the word needed is almost always *effect* (as in 'personal effects' or 'the damaging effects of war'). *Affect* as a noun has a narrow psychological meaning to do with emotional states (by way of which it is related to *affection*).

It is worth noting that *affect* as a verb is nearly always bland and almost meaningless. In 'The winter weather affected profits in the building division' (*The Times*) and 'The noise of the crowds affected his play' (*Daily Telegraph*), it is by no means clear whether the noise and weather helped or hindered or delayed or exacerbated the profits and play. A more precise word can almost always be found.

affinity denotes a mutual relationship. Therefore, strictly speaking, one should not speak of someone or something having an affinity for another, but rather should speak of an affinity with or between. When mutuality is not intended, 'sympathy' would be a better word. But it should also be noted that a number of authorities and many dictionaries no longer insist on this distinction.

affright. Note -*ff*-.

Afrikaans, Afrikaners. The first is a language, the second a group of people.

Afrikaners. See AFRIKAANS, AFRIKANERS.

agenda. Although a plural in Latin, *agenda* in English is singular. Its English plural is *agendas* (but see DATA).

aggravate in the sense of 'exasperate' has been with us at least since the early seventeenth century and has been opposed by grammarians for about as long. Strictly, *aggravate* means to make a bad situation worse. If you walk on a broken leg, you may aggravate the injury. People can never be aggravated, only circumstances. Fowler, who called objections to the looser usage a fetish, was no doubt right when he insisted the purists were fighting a battle that was already lost, but equally there is no real reason to use *aggravate* when 'annoy' will do.

aggression, aggressiveness. 'Aggression in US pays off for Tilling Group' (*Times* headline). *Aggression* always denotes hostility, which was not intended here. The writer of the headline meant to suggest only that the company had taken a determined and enterprising approach to the American market. The word he wanted was *aggressiveness*, which can denote either hostility or merely boldness and assertiveness.

aggressiveness. See AGGRESSION, AGGRESSIVENESS.

aid and abet. A tautological gift from the legal profession. The two words together tell us nothing that either doesn't say on its own. The only distinction is that *abet* is normally reserved for contexts involving criminal intent. Thus it would be careless to speak of a benefactor abetting the construction of a church or youth club. Other redundant expressions dear to lawyers include 'null and void', 'ways and means' and 'without let or hindrance'.

Aids is not correctly described as a disease. It is a medical condition. The term is short for acquired immune deficiency syndrome.

airlines. 'It is thought the company may also be in exploratory talks with another US carrier, Alaskan Airlines' (*The Times*). It's Alaska Airlines. 'It was found only a few miles from where a Swiss Air jet crashed two years ago' (*Boston Globe*). It's Swissair. Perhaps because they so commonly merge or change their names, airlines are often wrongly designated in newspaper reporting. The following are among the more commonly troublesome:

Aer Lingus

Aerolíneas Argentinas

AeroMexico

AeroPéru

Air-India (note hyphen)

AirTran Airlines (formerly ValuJet Airlines)

Alaska Airlines

All Nippon Airways (not *-lines*)

Delta Air Lines (note *Air Lines* two words)

Iberia Airlines (not Iberian)

Icelandair

Japan Airlines (*Airlines* one word, but JAL for the company's abbreviation)

KLM Royal Dutch Airlines (normally just KLM)

LanChile

Sabena Belgian World Airlines (normally just Sabena)

Scandinavian Airlines System (normally just SAS)

SriLankan Airlines

Swissair

United Airlines (*Airlines* one word, but UAL for the company's abbreviation)

US Airways (formerly USAir, one word)

Virgin Atlantic Airways

'Alas! poor Yorick! I knew him, Horatio', is the correct version of the quotation from *Hamlet*, which is often wrongly, and somewhat mysteriously, rendered as 'Alas poor Yorick, I knew him well'.

albumen, albumin. *Albumen* is the white of an egg; *albumin* is a protein within the albumen.

albumin. See ALBUMEN, ALBUMIN.

alias, alibi. Both words derive from the Latin root *alius* (meaning 'other'). *Alias* refers to an assumed name and pertains only to names. It would be incorrect to speak of an impostor passing himself off under the alias of being a doctor.

Alibi is a much more contentious word. In legal parlance it refers to a plea by an accused person that he was elsewhere at the time he was alleged to have committed a crime. More commonly it is used to mean any excuse. Fowler called this latter usage mischievous and pretentious, and most authorities agree with him. But Bernstein, while conceding that the usage is a casualism, contends that there is no other word that can quite convey the meaning of an excuse intended to transfer responsibility. Time will no doubt support him – many distinguished writers have used *alibi* in its more general, less fastidious sense – but for the moment all that can be said is that in the sense of a general excuse, many authorities consider *alibi* unacceptable.

alibi. See ALIAS, ALIBI.

allay, alleviate, assuage, relieve. *Alleviate* should suggest giving temporary relief without removing the underlying cause of a problem. It is close in meaning to 'ease', a fact obviously unknown to the writer of this sentence: 'It will ease the transit squeeze, but will not alleviate it' (*Chicago Tribune*). *Allay* and *assuage* both mean to put to rest or to pacify and are most often applied to fears. *Relieve* is the more general term and covers all these meanings.

allegory. See FABLE, PARABLE, ALLEGORY, MYTH.

alleviate. See ALLAY, ALLEVIATE, ASSUAGE, RELIEVE.

all intents and purposes is colourless, redundant and hackneyed. Almost any other expression would be an improvement. 'He is, to all intents and purposes, king of the island' (*Mail on Sunday*) would be instantly made better by changing the central phrase to 'in effect' or removing it altogether. If the phrase must be used at all, it can always be shorn of the last two words. 'To all intents' says as much as 'to all intents and purposes'.

all right. A sound case could be made for shortening *all right* to *alright*, as many informal users of English do already. Many other compounds beginning with *all* have been contracted without protest for centuries, among them *already, almost, altogether* and even *alone*, which originally was *all one*. And certainly even in the most respected papers *alright* crops up from time to time, as here: 'You came away thinking: "The guy's alright"' (*Observer*); 'The engine cuts out and someone says: "Poor chap, I hope he will be alright"' (*The Times*). English, however, is a slow and fickle tongue, and *alright* continues to be looked on as illiterate and unacceptable, and consequently it ought never to appear in serious writing.

All Souls College, Oxford. Not *Souls'*, etc.

all time. Many authorities object to this expression in constructions such as 'She was almost certainly the greatest female sailor of all time' (*Daily Telegraph*) on the grounds that *all time* extends to the future as well as the past and we cannot possibly know what lies ahead. A no less pertinent consideration is that such assessments, as in the example just cited, are bound to be hopelessly subjective and therefore have no place in any measured argument. For a similar problem with futurity, see also EVER.

allusion. 'When the speaker happened to name Mr Gladstone, the allusion was received with loud cheers' (cited by Fowler). The word is not, as many suppose, a more impressive synonym for 'reference'. When you allude to something, you do not specifically mention it, but leave it to the reader to deduce the subject. Thus it would be correct to write, 'In an allusion to the President, he said: "Some people make better oil men than politicians"'. The word is closer in meaning to 'implication' or 'suggestion'.

along with. See TOGETHER WITH, ALONG WITH.

altercation. 'Three youths were injured in the altercation' (*Chicago Tribune*). No one gets physically hurt in an altercation. It is a heated exchange of words and nothing more.

although. See THOUGH, ALTHOUGH.

ambidextrous. Not -*erous*.

ambiguous, equivocal. Both mean vague and open to more than one interpretation. But whereas an ambiguous statement may be vague by accident or by intent, an equivocal one is calculatedly unclear.

amid, among. *Among* applies to things that can be separated and counted, *amid* to things that cannot. Rescuers might search among survivors, but amid wreckage.

among. See AMID, AMONG; BETWEEN, AMONG.

amoral, immoral. *Amoral* describes matters in which questions of morality do not arise or are disregarded; *immoral* applies to things that are evil.

an. See A, AN.

and. The belief that *and* should not be used to begin a sentence is without foundation. And that's all there is to it.

A thornier problem is seen here: 'The group has interests in Germany, Australia, Japan and intends to expand into North America next year' (*The Times*). This is what Fowler called a bastard enumeration and Bernstein, with more delicacy, called a series out of control. The defect is that the closing clause ('intends to expand into North America next year') does not belong to the series that precedes it. It is a separate thought. The sentence should read: 'The group has interests in Germany, Australia and Japan, and intends to expand into North America next year'. (Note that the inclusion of a comma after 'Japan' helps to signal that the series has ended and a new clause is beginning.)

The same problem is seen here: 'Department of Trade officials, tax and accountancy experts were to be involved at an early stage in the investigation' (*Guardian*). *And* here is being asked to do two jobs at once: to mark the end of a series and to join 'tax' and 'accountancy' to 'experts'. It isn't up to it. The sentence needs to say: 'Department of Trade officials and tax and accountancy experts . . .'. This reluctance by writers to supply a second *and* is common but always misguided.

Andersen, Hans Christian, for the Danish writer of children's tales. Not *-son*.

androgenous, androgynous. The first applies to the production of male offspring; the second means having both male and female characteristics.

androgynous. See ANDROGENOUS, ANDROGYNOUS.

and which. 'The rights issue, the largest so far this year and which was not unexpected, will be used to fund expansion plans' (*The Times*). *And which* should almost always be preceded by a parallel *which*. The sentence above would be unexceptionable, and would read more smoothly, if it were changed to: 'The rights issue, which was the largest so far this year and which was not unexpected . . .'. Occasionally the need for euphony may excuse the absence of the first *which*, but such instances are rare and usually the omission is no more than a sign of slipshod writing. The stricture applies equally to such constructions as *and that, and who, but which* and *but who*. (See also THAT, WHICH.)

annex, annexe. In British usage, *annex* is the verb spelling and *annexe* the noun spelling. In American usage, *annex* is the preferred spelling for both.

annexe. See ANNEX, ANNEXE.

anno Domini (Latin), in the year of the Lord (cap. 'D' only). (See also AD.)

annual, a year. It is surprising how often both crop up in the same sentence, as here: 'Beecham Soft Drinks, which will have joint annual sales of £200 million a year . . .' (*Guardian*). Choose one or the other obviously.

another. 'Some 400 workers were laid off at the Liverpool factory and another 150 in Bristol' (*Daily Telegraph*). Strictly speaking, *another* should be used to equate two things of equal size and type. In this instance it would be correct only if 400 workers were being laid off in Bristol also. It would be better to write 'and 150 more [or others] in Bristol'.

antecedence, antecedents. *Antecedence* means precedence; *antecedents* are ancestors or other things that have gone before.

antecedents. See ANTECEDENCE, ANTECEDENTS.

antennae, antennas. Either is correct as the plural of *antenna*, but generally *antennae* is preferred for living organisms ('a beetle's antennae') and *antennas* for man-made objects ('radio antennas made possible the discovery of quarks').

antennas. See ANTENNAE, ANTENNAS.

anticipate. 'First-year losses in the video division were greater than anticipated' (*The Times*). To anticipate something is to look ahead to it and prepare for it, not to make a reasonable estimate, as was apparently intended here. A tennis player who anticipates his opponent's next shot doesn't just guess where it is going to go, he is there to meet it. In the example above, the use of the word is contradictory. If the company had anticipated the losses, it wouldn't have found them larger than expected.

anxious. Since *anxious* comes from *anxiety*, it should contain some connotation of being worried or fearful and not merely eager or expectant. You may be anxious to put some unpleasant task behind you, but, unless you have invested money in it, you are unlikely to be anxious to see a new play.

any. A tricky word at times, even for the experts: 'This paper isn't very good, but neither is any of the others in this miserable subject' (Howard, *The State of the Language*). A useful principle is to make the verb always correspond to the complement. Thus: 'neither is any other' or 'neither are any of the others'.

anybody, anyone, anything, anyway, anywhere. *Anything* and *anywhere* are always one word. The others are normally one word except when the emphasis is on the second element (e.g., 'He received three job offers, but any one would have suited him').

Anybody and *anyone* are singular and should be followed by singular pronouns and verbs. A common fault – so common, in fact, that some no longer consider it a fault – is seen here: 'Anyone can relax, so long as they don't care whether they or anyone else ever actually gets anything done' (*Observer*). So long as they gets anything done? The problem, clearly, is that a plural pronoun ('they') is being attached to a singular verb ('gets'). Such constructions may in fact be fully defensible, at least some of the time, though you should at least know why you are breaking a rule when you break it. For a full discussion, see NUMBER (4).

any more, any time. Both are always two words.

anyone. See ANYBODY, ANYONE, ANYTHING, ANYWAY, ANYWHERE.

anything. See ANYBODY, ANYONE, ANYTHING, ANYWAY, ANY-
WHERE.

any time. See ANY MORE, ANY TIME.

anyway. See ANYBODY, ANYONE, ANYTHING, ANYWAY, ANY-
WHERE.

anywhere. See ANYBODY, ANYONE, ANYTHING, ANYWAY, ANY-
WHERE.

Apennines for the Italian mountain range. Note *-nn-* in middle.

appendices, appendixes. Either is correct.

appendixes. See APPENDICES, APPENDIXES.

appraise, apprise. 'No decision is likely, he said, until they had
been appraised of the damage' (*Sunday Times*). The word wanted
here was *apprise*, which means to inform. *Appraise* means to assess
or evaluate. An insurance assessor appraises damage and apprises
owners.

appreciate has a slightly more specific meaning than writers
sometimes give it. If you appreciate something, you value it ('I
appreciate your concern') or you understand it sympathetically
('I appreciate your predicament'). But when there is no sense of
sympathy or value (as in 'I appreciate what you are saying, but I
don't agree with it'), 'understand' or 'recognize' or the like would
be better words.

apprise. See APPRAISE, APPRISE.

approximate means 'near to', so *very approximate* ought to mean
'very near to'. Yet when most people speak of a very approximate
estimate, they mean a very tentative one, not a very close one.

Gowers, in *The Complete Plain Words*, roundly criticized the usage as loose and misleading, but Fowler classed it among his 'sturdy indefensibles' – words and phrases that are clearly illogical, and perhaps even lamentable, but are now so firmly entrenched that objections become pointless. In this, I believe, Fowler was right.

Where the authorities do find common ground is in the belief that *approximate* and *approximate to* are cumbersome and nearly always better replaced by something shorter. No need to write 'We were approximately 12 miles from home' when you could make it 'about' or 'almost' or 'nearly'.

a priori, prima facie. Both generally refer to evidence and thus are sometimes confused. *Prima facie* means 'at first sight' or 'on the surface of it', and refers to matters in which not all of the evidence has been collected but in which such evidence as there is points to certain conclusions. *A priori* refers to conclusions drawn from assumptions rather than experience.

apt. See LIABLE, LIKELY, APT, PRONE.

Aran Island and **Aran Islands** (Ireland) but *Isle of Arran* (Scotland). The sweater is spelled *Aran*.

Aran Islands. See ARAN ISLAND and ARAN ISLANDS.

arbitrate, mediate. The functions of these two words differ more than is sometimes appreciated. Arbitrators are like judges in that they are appointed to hear evidence and then to make a decision. Mediators are more like negotiators in that they shuttle between opposing sides trying to work out a compromise or settlement. They do not make judgements.

Difficulties sometimes also arise in distinguishing between an arbitrator and an arbiter. Whereas an arbitrator is appointed, an arbiter is someone whose opinions are valued but in whom there is no vested authority. Fowler summed up the distinction neatly: 'An arbiter acts arbitrarily; an arbitrator must not'.

argot. See JARGON, ARGOT, LINGUA FRANCA.

aroma does not apply to any smell, but only to pleasant ones. Thus 'the pungent aroma of a cattleyard' (*Washington Post*) is wrong.

Arran, Isle of. See ARAN ISLAND and ARAN ISLANDS.

artefact, artifact. The first spelling is generally preferred in Britain, the second in America, but either is correct. In either case, it is something shaped by human hand and not merely any very old object, as was apparently thought here: 'The team found bones and other artefacts at the site' (*Guardian*). Bones are not artefacts. The word is related to *artifice, artificial* and *artisan*, all of which imply a human contribution.

artifact. See ARTEFACT, ARTIFACT.

as. See LIKE, AS.

as ... as. 'Housing conditions in Toxteth may be as bad, if not worse than, any in Britain' (*Observer*). The problem here is what is termed an incomplete alternative comparison. If we remove the 'if not worse' phrase from the sentence, the problem becomes clearer: 'Housing conditions in Toxteth may be as bad ... than any in Britain'. The writer has left the 'as bad' phrase dangling incompleted. The sentence should say 'as bad *as*, if not worse than, any in Britain'.

assiduous. See ACIDULOUS, ASSIDUOUS.

assuage. See ALLAY, ALLEVIATE, ASSUAGE, RELIEVE.

assume, presume. The two words are often so close in meaning as to be indistinguishable, but in some contexts they do allow a fine distinction to be made. *Assume*, in the sense of 'to suppose', normally means to put forth a realistic hypothesis, something that can be taken as probable ('I assume we will arrive by midnight'). *Presume* has more of an air of sticking one's neck out, of making an assertion that may be contentious ('I presume we have met before?'). But in most instances the two words can be used interchangeably.

as to whether. *Whether* alone is sufficient.

attain. 'The uncomfortable debt level attained by the end of the financial year has now been eased' (*The Times*). *Attain*, like 'achieve' and 'accomplish', suggests the reaching of a desired goal – hardly the sense intended here. It would have been better to change the word (to 'prevailing', for example) or, in this instance, to delete it.

auger, augur. 'The results do not auger well for the President in the forthcoming mid-term elections' (*Guardian*). Wrong. *Auger* is not a verb; it is a drilling tool. To foretell or betoken, the sense intended in the example, is to *augur*, with a 'u'. The two words are not related. In fact, until relatively recent times an auger was called a nauger.

augur. See AUGER, AUGUR.

auspicious does not mean simply special or memorable. It means propitious, promising, of good omen.

autarchy, autarky. The first means absolute power, an autocracy; the second denotes self-sufficiency. Some style books – *The Oxford Dictionary for Writers and Editors* and *The Economist Pocket Style Book*, for instance – are at pains to point out the distinction, and it is worth noting that the two words do spring from different Greek roots. But the same books usually fail to observe that neither word is comfortably understood by most general readers, and that in almost every instance their English synonyms would bring an improvement in comprehension, if not in elegance.

autarky. See AUTARCHY, AUTARKY.

autobahn (German), express motorway. The plural is *autobahns* or *Autobahnen*.

autostrada (Italian), express motorway. The plural is *autostrade*.

auxiliary. Not *-ll-*.

avant-garde. Note hyphen.

avenge, revenge. Generally, *avenge* indicates the settling of a score or the redressing of an injustice. It is more dispassionate than *revenge*, which indicates retaliation taken largely for the sake of personal satisfaction.

average. 'The average wage in Australia is now about £150 a week, though many people earn much more' (*The Times*). And many earn much less. That is what makes £150 the average. When expressing an average figure, it is generally unnecessary, and sometimes fatuous, to elaborate on its exceptions. (See also MEAN, MEDIAN, MIDRANGE, MODE.)

averse. See ADVERSE, AVERSE.

avocado. The plural is *avocados*.

awake. See AWOKE, AWAKED, AWAKENED.

awakened. See AWOKE, AWAKED, AWAKENED.

awhile. See A WHILE, AWHILE.

a while, awhile. To write 'for awhile' is wrong because the idea of 'for' is implicit in *awhile*. Write either 'I will stay here for a while' (two words) or 'I will stay here awhile' (one word).

awoke, awaked, awakened. Two common problems are worth noting:

1. *Awoken*, though much used, is generally considered not standard. Thus this sentence from an Agatha Christie novel (cited by Partridge) is wrong: 'I was awoken by that rather flashy young woman'. Make it *awakened*.

2. As a past participle, *awaked* is preferable to *awoke*. Thus, 'He had awaked at midnight' and not 'He had woke [or awoke] at midnight'. But if ever in doubt about the past tense, you will never be wrong if you use *awakened*.

axel, axle. An axel is a jump in ice skating; an axle is a rod connecting two wheels.

axle. See AXEL, AXLE.

a year. See ANNUAL, A YEAR.

Ayers Rock (no apos.) for the Australian eminence. However, the formal name now is Uluru.

B

bacteria is plural. A single organism is a bacterium. Note also that bacteria are not at all the same as viruses. Bacteria are living single-celled organisms with the capability to reproduce independently. Viruses are much smaller and capable of reproducing only after invading a living cell; they are not independent living organisms.

bail, bale. *Bail* is a prisoner's bond, the pieces that rest atop the stumps in cricket and the act of scooping water. *Bale* is a bundle, as of cotton or hay. You bail out a boat, but bale out of an aircraft. A malicious person wears a baleful expression.

bait, bate. 'Robin's exploits were listened to with baited breath' (*Mail on Sunday*). Unless Robin's listeners were hoping to catch fish, their breath was *bated*. The word is a cousin of *abated*.

bale. See BAIL, BALE.

balk, baulk. Either spelling is correct.

banzai, **bonsai.** The first is a Japanese war cry; the second is a type of Japanese gardening centred on miniature trees.

barbaric, barbarous. *Barbaric*, properly used, emphasizes crudity and a lack of civilizing influence. A sharpened stick might be considered a barbaric implement of war. *Barbarous* stresses cruelty and harshness and usually contains at least a hint of moral condemnation, as in 'barbarous ignorance' or 'barbarous treatment'.

barbarous. See BARBARIC, BARBAROUS.

barbecue is the only acceptable spelling in serious writing. Any journalist or other formal user of English who believes that the word is spelled *barbeque* or, worse still, *bar-b-q* is not ready for unsupervised employment.

barrier. 'BTR's profits this week went through the £1bn pre-tax profits barrier' (*Independent*). Even in the broadest figurative sense, a *barrier* should suggest some kind of obstacle or impediment – and clearly there is nothing stopping any company from piling up any level of profit. If the urge to employ a metaphor is irresistible, try 'milestone'.

basically. The trouble with this word is that in most contexts it is basically unnecessary, as here.

basis. Almost always a sure indicator of wordiness, as here: 'Det. Chief Supt. Peter Topping . . . said he would review the search on a day-to-day basis' (*Independent*). Why not make it 'would review the search daily' and save five words?

bate. See BAIT, BATE.

bathos. From the Greek *bathus*, meaning 'deep', *bathos* can be used to indicate the lowest point or nadir, or triteness and insincerity. But its usual use is in describing an abrupt descent from an elevated position to the commonplace. It is not the opposite of pathos, which is to do with feelings of pity or sympathy.

baulk. See BALK, BAULK.

BC always goes after the year (42 BC) and is usually set in small caps. (See also AD.)

be (with a participle). Almost always a wordy way of getting your point across, as here: 'He will be joining the board of directors in March' (*The Times*). Quicker to say: 'He will join the board of directors in March'.

Becher's Brook is the spelling of the famous and formidable jump on the Grand National course.

before, prior to. There is no difference between these two except length and that *prior to* has a certain affectedness. To paraphrase Bernstein, if you would use 'posterior to' instead of 'after', then by all means use *prior to* instead of *before*.

behalf. A useful distinction exists between *on behalf of* and *in behalf of*. The first means acting as a representative, as when a lawyer enters a plea on behalf of a client, and often denotes a formal relationship. *In behalf of* indicates a closer or more sympathetic role and means acting as a friend or defender.

'I spoke on your behalf' means that I represented you when you were absent. 'I spoke in your behalf' means that I supported you or defended you.

behove. An archaic word, but still sometimes a useful one. Two points need to be made:

1. The word means necessary or contingent, but is sometimes wrongly used for 'becomes', particularly with the adverb 'ill', as in 'It ill behoves any man responsible for policy to think how best to make political propaganda' (cited by Gowers).

2. It should be used only impassively and with the subject 'it'. 'The circumstances behove us to take action' is wrong. Make it, 'It behoves us in the circumstances to take action'.

The American spelling is *behoove*.

beleaguered. Not -*ured*.

belles-lettres describes writing having a literary or aesthetic, as opposed to purely informational, value. The word is usually treated as a plural, but may be used as a singular. For reasons unconnected to logic, the hyphen is lost and the word itself contracted in the related terms *belletrist*, *belletrism* and *belletristic*.

bellwether. Not -*weather*. *Wether* is an old word for sheep. A bellwether is a sheep that has a bell hung from its neck, by which means it leads the herd from one pasture to another. In general use, it means one that leads or shows the way. A bellwether stock is one that is customarily at the head of the pack. It does not mean a harbinger or foreteller of events.

beluga is a type of sturgeon, and not a manufacturer or producer of caviare, as is sometimes thought, so the word should not be capitalized (except of course at the start of a sentence).

benzene, benzine. Both are liquid hydrocarbons commonly used as solvents. *Benzene* is primarily associated with the production of plastics, while *benzine* most often is encountered as a solvent used in dry-cleaning establishments. At all events, they are quite different substances and not merely alternative spellings of a single compound.

benzine. See BENZENE, BENZINE.

bereft. 'Many children leave school altogether bereft of mathematical skills' (*The Times*, cited by Kingsley Amis in *The State of the Language*). To be bereft of something is not to lack it but to be dispossessed of it. A spinster is not bereft of a husband, but a widow is (the word is the past participle of *bereave*).

besides means 'also' or 'in addition to', not 'alternatively'. Partridge cites this incorrect use: '. . . the wound must have been made by something besides the handle of the gear-lever'. Make it 'other than'.

besiege. Not -*ei*-.

between, among. A few authorities continue to insist that *between* applies to two things only and *among* to more than two, so that we should speak of dividing some money between the two of us, but among the four of us. That is useful advice as far as it goes, but it doesn't always go very far. It would be absurd, for instance, to say that Chicago is among New York, Los Angeles and Houston. More logically, *between* should be applied to reciprocal arrangements (a treaty between the UK, the US and Canada) and *among* to collective arrangements (trade talks among the members of the European Union).

A separate, common problem with *between* is seen here: 'He said the new salaries were between 30 to 40 per cent more than the average paid by other retailers' (*Independent*). Something can only be between one thing and another. Thus you should say either 'between 30 and 40 per cent' or 'from 30 to 40 per cent'.

between you and I. John Simon called this 'a grammatical error of unsurpassable grossness'. It is perhaps enough to say that it is very common and it is always wrong. The rule is that the object of a preposition should always be in the accusative. More simply, we don't say 'between you and I' for the same reason that we don't say 'give that book to I' or 'as Tom was saying to she only yesterday'. A similar gaffe is seen here: 'He leaves behind 79 astronauts, many young enough to be the children of he and the others . . .' (*Daily Mail*). Make it 'of him'.

Big Ben, strictly speaking, is not the famous clock on the Houses of Parliament, but just the great hour bell. The formal name of the clock, for what it is worth, is the clock on St Stephen's Tower on the Palace of Westminster.

bilateral. See UNILATERAL, BILATERAL, MULTILATERAL.

bimonthly, biweekly and similar designations are almost always ambiguous. It is far better to say 'every two months', 'twice a month', etc., as appropriate.

Bishopsgate for the area of the City of London. Note *-ps-*.

biweekly. See BIMONTHLY, BIWEEKLY.

blatant, flagrant. The words are not quite synonymous. Something that is blatant is glaringly obvious and contrived ('a blatant lie') or wilfully obnoxious ('blatant electioneering') or both. Something that is flagrant is shocking and reprehensible ('a flagrant miscarriage of justice'). If I tell you that I regularly travel to the moon, that is a blatant lie, not a flagrant one. If you set fire to my house, that is a flagrant act, not a blatant one.

blazon. '[She] blazoned a trail in the fashion world which others were quick to follow' (*Sunday Times*). Trails are blazed. To blazon means to display or proclaim in an ostentatious manner.

blueprint as a metaphor for a design or plan is much overworked. If the temptation to use it is irresistible, at least remember that a blueprint is a completed plan, not a preliminary one.

bogey, bogie, bogy. A bogey is one stroke over par in golf, as well as an indelicate term for what is found up the nose; a bogie is a wheeled undercarriage, as on a train; and bogy is an alternative spelling for either. The normal spelling for the imaginary monster is bogeyman.

bogie. See BOGEY, BOGIE, BOGY.

bogy. See BOGEY, BOGIE, BOGY.

bonsai. See BANZAI, BONSAI.

bon vivant, bon viveur. The first is a person who enjoys good food, the second a person who lives well.

bon viveur. See BON VIVANT, BON VIVEUR.

born, borne. Both are past particles of the verb *bear*, but by convention they are used in slightly different ways. *Born* is limited to the idea of birth ('He was born in December'). *Borne* should be used for the sense of supporting or tolerating ('She has borne the burden with dignity'), but is also used to refer to giving birth in active constructions ('She has borne three children') and in passive constructions followed by 'by' ('The three children borne by her . . .').

borne. See BORN, BORNE.

both. Three small problems to note:

1. *Both* should not be used to describe more than two things. Partridge cites a passage in which a woman is said to have 'a shrewd common sense . . . both in speech, deed and dress'. Delete *both*.

2. Sometimes it appears superfluously: '. . . and they both went to the same school, Charterhouse' (*Observer*). Either delete *both* or make it '. . . they both went to Charterhouse'.

3. Sometimes it is misused for 'each'. To say that there is a supermarket on both sides of the street suggests that it is somehow straddling the roadway. Say either that there is a supermarket on each side of the street or that there are supermarkets on both sides. (See also EACH.)

both . . . and. 'He was both deaf to argument and entreaty' (cited by Gowers). The rule involved here is that of correlative conjunctions, which states that in a sentence of this type *both* and *and* should link grammatically similar entities. If *both* is followed immediately by a verb, *and* should also be followed immediately by a verb. If *both* immediately precedes a noun, then so should *and*. In the example above, however, *both* is followed by an adjective (deaf) and *and* by a noun (entreaty).

The sentence needs to be recast, either as 'He was deaf to both argument [noun] and entreaty [noun]' or as 'He was deaf both to argument [preposition and noun] and to entreaty [preposition and noun]'.

The rule holds true equally for other such pairs: 'not only . . . but also', 'either . . . or', and 'neither . . . nor'.

bottleneck, as Gowers notes, is a useful, if sometimes overworked, metaphor to indicate a point of constriction. But it should not be forgotten that it is a metaphor and therefore capable of cracking when put under too much pressure. To speak, for instance, of 'a worldwide bottleneck' or 'a growing bottleneck' sounds a note of absurdity. Bottlenecks, even figurative ones, don't grow and they don't encompass the earth.

bouillabaisse. Not *-illi-*.

bravado should not be confused with bravery. It is a swaggering or boastful display of boldness, often adopted to disguise an underlying timidity. It is, in short, a false bravery and there is nothing courageous about it.

breach, breech. Frequently confused. *Breach* describes an infraction or a gap. It should always suggest break, a word to which it is related. *Breech* applies to the rear or lower portion of things. The main expressions are breach of faith (or promise), breech birth, breeches buoy, breechcloth and breech-loading gun.

breech. See BREACH, BREECH.

Britannia, Britannic, but *Brittany.* The song is 'Rule, Britannia', with a comma.

Britannic. See BRITANNIA, BRITANNIC.

British Guiana is the former name of the South American country now known as Guyana.

BSE is short for bovine spongiform encephalopathy.

buenos días (for good-day or hello in Spanish), but *buenas* (not -*os*) *noches* (good-night) and *buenas tardes* (good-afternoon).

buffalo. The plural can be either *buffalo* or *buffaloes*.

buoy. Though this book does not normally address matters of pronunciation, and though it is intended primarily for users of British English, I cannot resist pointing out to my fellow Americans, and any who may be influenced by them, that the increasing tendency to pronounce this word *boo-ee* is mistaken and misguided. Unless you would say *boo-ee-ant* for *buoyant*, please return to pronouncing it *boy*.

burgeon does not mean merely to expand or thrive. It means to bud or sprout, to come into being. For something to burgeon, it must be new. Thus it would be correct to talk about the burgeoning talent of a precocious youth, but to write of 'the ever-burgeoning population of Cairo' (*Daily Telegraph*) is wrong. Cairo's population has been growing for centuries, and nothing, in any case, is ever-burgeoning.

but used negatively after a pronoun presents a problem that has confounded careful users for generations. Do you say, 'Everyone but him had arrived' or 'Everyone but he had arrived'? The authorities themselves are divided.

Some regard *but* as a preposition and put the pronoun in the accusative – i.e., me, her, him or them. So just as we say, 'Give it to her' or 'between you and me', we should say, 'Everyone but him had arrived'.

Others argue that *but* is a conjunction and that the pronoun should be nominative (I, she, he or they), as if the sentence were saying, 'Everyone had arrived, but he had not'.

The answer perhaps is to regard *but* sometimes as a conjunction and sometimes as a preposition. Two rough rules should help.

1. If the pronoun appears at the end of the sentence, you can

always use the accusative and be on firm ground. Thus, 'Nobody knew but her'; 'Everyone had eaten but him'.

2. When the pronoun appears earlier in the sentence, it is almost always better to put it in the nominative, as in 'No one but he had seen it'. The one exception is when the pronoun is influenced by a preceding preposition, but such constructions are relatively rare and often clumsy. Two examples might be: 'Between no one but them was there any bitterness'; 'To everyone but him life was a mystery'. (See also THAN (3).)

C

caddie, caddy. A caddie is a golfer's assistant; a caddy is a container for storing tea.

caddy. See CADDIE, CADDY.

Caesarean, not *-ian*, remains the preferred spelling for the form of childbirth properly known as a Caesarean section, as well as for references to Roman emperors named Caesar.

Caius, the Cambridge college, is formally Gonville and Caius College. Caius is pronounced *keys*.

calligraphy. 'Both ransom notes have been forwarded to calligraphy experts in Rome' (*Daily Mail*). The writer meant 'graphologists' or 'graphology experts'. Calligraphy is an art.

camellia for the flower. Not *camelia*.

can, may. *Can* applies to what is possible and *may* to what is permissible. You can drive your car the wrong way down a one-way street, but you may not. Despite the simplicity of the rule, errors are common, even among experts. Here is William Safire, the *New York Times* usage authority, on the pronunciation of *junta*: 'The worst mistake is to mix languages. You cannot say "joonta" and you cannot say "hunta".' But you can and quite easily. What Mr Safire meant was that you may not or should not or ought not.

cannot help but is an increasingly common construction, and perhaps now may be said to carry the weight of idiom, but it is also worth noting that it is both unnecessarily wordy and a little irregular. 'You cannot help but notice what a bad name deregulation has with voters' (*Economist*) would be better (or at least more conventionally phrased) as either 'You cannot help notice . . .' or 'You cannot but notice . . .'.

canvas, canvass. The first is the fabric; the second is a verb meaning to solicit, especially for votes.

canvass. See CANVAS, CANVASS.

capital, capitol. *Capitol* always applies to a building, usually the place where legislatures gather in the United States. It is always capitalized when referring to the domed building in Washington, DC, housing the US Congress. In all other senses, *capital* is the invariable spelling.

capitol. See CAPITAL, CAPITOL.

carat, caret. *Carat* is a unit of measurement for precious stones (where it indicates weight) and gold (where it indicates purity); *caret* is an insertion mark (∧) associated with proofreading. The American spelling of *carat* is *karat*.

carbon dioxide, carbon monoxide. *Carbon dioxide* is the gas we exhale when we breathe; *carbon monoxide* is the highly poisonous gas associated with car exhausts.

carbon monoxide. See CARBON DIOXIDE, CARBON MONOXIDE.

cardinal numbers, ordinal numbers. *Cardinal numbers* are those that denote size but not rank: 1, 2, 3, etc. *Ordinal numbers* are those that denote position: first, second, third, etc.

careen, career. Occasionally confused when describing runaway vehicles and the like. *Careen* should convey the idea of swaying or tilting dangerously. If all you mean is uncontrolled movement, use *career*.

career. See CAREEN, CAREER.

caret. See CARAT, CARET.

Catharine's, Catherine's. The Cambridge college is St Catharine's; the Oxford college is St Catherine's.

Catherine's. See CATHARINE'S, CATHERINE'S.

ceiling, floor. *Ceiling* used figuratively in the sense of an upper limit is a handy word, but, like many other handy words, is apt to be overused. When you do employ it figuratively, you should never forget that its literal meaning is always lurking in the background, ready to spring forward and make an embarrassment of your metaphor, as in this memorable headline from the *Daily Gulf Times*: 'Oil ministers want to stick to ceiling'.

Floor in the sense of a lower limit is, of course, equally likely to result in incongruities. Occasionally the two words get mixed together, as in this perplexing sentence cited by both Howard and Fowler: 'The effect of this announcement is that the total figure of £410 million can be regarded as a floor as well as a ceiling'. (See also TARGET.)

celebrant, celebrator. 'All this is music to the ears of James Bond fan club members . . . and to other celebrants who descend on New Orleans each Nov. 11 . . .' (*The New York Times*). Celebrants take part in religious ceremonies. Those who gather for purposes of revelry are celebrators.

celebrator. See CELEBRANT, CELEBRATOR.

Celeste, Mary. The *Mary Celeste*, an American brigantine whose passengers and crew mysteriously disappeared during a crossing of the Atlantic in 1872, is sometimes used metaphorically and almost always is misspelled, as here: 'At last, the sound of people in the City's Marie Celeste' (*Daily Mail*). Make it *Mary*.

celibacy. 'He claimed he had remained celibate throughout the four-year marriage' (*Daily Telegraph*). Celibacy does not, as is generally supposed, indicate abstinence from sexual relations. It means only to be unmarried, particularly if as a result of a religious vow. A married man cannot be celibate, but he may be chaste.

cement, concrete. The two are not interchangeable. Cement is a constituent of concrete, which also contains sand, gravel and crushed rock.

cemetery. Not *-ary*.

Centers for Disease Control and Prevention is the full name of the US institution that deals with matters of public health. Note the plural *Centers*.

centre round or **around.** 'Their argument centres around the Foreign Intelligence Surveillance Act' (*The Times*). *Centre* indicates a point, and a point cannot encircle anything. Make it 'centre on' or 'revolve around'.

centrifugal/centripetal force. Centrifugal force is to pull away from; centripetal force is to draw towards.

centripetal force. See CENTRIFUGAL/CENTRIPETAL FORCE.

chafe, chaff. The one may lead to the other, but their meanings are distinct. To chafe means to make sore or worn by rubbing (or, figuratively, to annoy or irritate). To chaff means to tease goodnaturedly. A person who is excessively chaffed is likely to grow chafed.

chaff. See CHAFE, CHAFF.

chamois. The plural is also *chamois*, for both the antelope and the cloth for wiping cars.

chilblain. Not *chill-*.

children's is the only possible spelling of the possessive form of children. Yet errors abound, as here: 'He is also the current presenter of the BBC1 childrens' programme "Saturday Superstore"' (*Observer*). But that error is at least half a grade better than those in which no punctuation at all is employed, as with Boots and Tesco advertising 'childrens clothes', W. H. Smith offering 'childrens books' and Cadbury holding an annual competition of 'childrens art'. The error is a sign of fundamental illiteracy and to be deplored at every appearance. (See also MEN'S, WOMEN'S; POSSESSIVES.)

choose. See OPT, CHOOSE.

chord, cord. A chord is a group of musical notes or a type of arc in geometry; a cord is a length of rope or similar material of twisted strands, or a stack of wood. You speak with your vocal cords.

Christ Church, Christchurch. Christ Church is the spelling and full name of the Oxford college (i.e., not *Christ Church College*). The communities in New Zealand and England are Christchurch.

chronic. See ACUTE, CHRONIC.

Cincinnati for the frequently misspelled city in Ohio, US.

CinemaScope is the correct spelling for the wide-screen film system.

circumstances, in the and **under the.** A useful distinction can be drawn between the two. *In the circumstances* should indicate merely that a situation exists: 'In the circumstances, I began to feel worried'. *Under the circumstances* should denote a situation in which action is necessitated or inhibited: 'Under the circumstances, I had no choice but to leave'.

claim. Properly, *claim* means to demand recognition of a right. You claim something that you wish to call your own – an inheritance, a lost possession, a piece of land. But increasingly it is used in the sense of assert or contend, as here: 'They claim that no one will be misled by the advertisement' (*Boston Globe*).

For years authorities decried this looser usage, insisting we replace *claim* in such constructions with 'assert', 'declare', 'maintain', 'contend' or some other less objectionable verb, and for years hardly anyone heeded them. The battle, I think, is now over. Even Fowler, who disliked the looser usage, eventually conceded that 'there is no doubt a vigour about *claim* – a pugnacity almost – that makes such words [as 'assert', etc.] seem tame by comparison'.

So use the word freely if you wish, but bear in mind that there are occasions when *claim* is clearly out of place, as in this headline from a newspaper in Hawaii (cited by Fowler): 'Oahu barmaid claims rape'. The imputation seems to be that the unfortunate woman has either committed a rape or has taken one as an entitlement. Whichever, the choice of word is regrettable, to say the very least.

clamour but *clamorous.*

clichés. 'A week may be a long time in politics. But it's a light year in the global economy' (*Observer*); 'Lawyers were last night considering seeking an injunction for the book, which was selling like hot cakes in London bookshops over the weekend' (*Independent*). Clichés are sometimes the most economical way of expressing a complicated notion ('to hang by a thread', 'the tip of the iceberg', 'to point the finger'), but more often they are simply a sign of inert and unthinking writing and editing. It is not too much to say that in serious newspapers no story should begin by noting that a week is a long time in politics and nothing should ever sell like hot cakes, even hot cakes. For a quite separate problem with the first example above, see also LIGHT YEARS.

climactic, climatic, climacteric. *Climactic* means appearing at a climax ('the climactic scene in a movie'); *climatic* means having to do with climate and weather ('the climatic conditions produced rain'); *climacteric* is a noun signifying a time of important change and is most commonly applied to menopause.

climb up, climb down. *Climb down*, as purists sometimes point out, is a patent contradiction. But there you are. Idiom has embraced it, as it has many other patent absurdities, and there is no gainsaying it now. *Climb up*, on the other hand, is always redundant when *climb* is used transitively – which is to say most of the time. An exceptional intransitive use of *climb* would be: 'After each descent, we rested for a while before climbing up again'. But in a sentence such as 'He climbed up the ladder', the *up* does nothing but take up space. (See also PHRASAL VERBS and UP.)

close proximity is inescapably tautological. Make it 'near' or 'close to'.

coelacanth for the type of fish. Pronounced *see-luh-kanth*.

co-equal. 'In almost every other regard the two are co-equal' (*Guardian*). A fatuous term. *Co-* adds nothing to *equal* that *equal* doesn't already say alone.

cognomen applies only to a person's surname, not to his or her full name or given names. Except jocularly, it is generally better avoided.

cognoscenti, meaning people who are especially well informed or of elevated taste, is plural. For a single well-informed person, the word is *cognoscente*.

colic but *colicky*.

coliseum, Colosseum. The first applies to any large amphitheatre; the second describes a particular amphitheatre in Rome.

collapsible. Not *-able*.

collectives. Deciding whether to treat nouns of multitude – words like 'majority', 'flock', 'army', 'Government', 'group', 'crowd' and the like – as singulars or plurals is entirely a matter of the sense you intend to convey. Although some authorities have tried to fix rules, such undertakings are almost always futile. On the whole, Americans lean to the singular and Britons to the plural, often in ways that would strike the other as absurd (compare the American 'The couple was married in 1978' with the British 'England are to play Hungary in their next match'). A common fault is to flounder about between singular and plural, as here: 'The group, which *has* been expanding vigorously abroad, *are* more optimistic about the second half' (*The Times*). Even Samuel Johnson stumbled when he wrote that he knew of no nation 'that *has* preserved *their* words and phases from mutability'. In both sentences, the italicized pairs of words should be either singular both times or plural both times.

collide, collision. 'The lorry had broken down when another car was in collision with it' (*Standard*). Such sentences, which are common in newspapers, are wrong in two ways. First, a collision can occur only when two or more *moving* objects come together. If a car runs into a broken-down lorry, a wall, a lamp-post or any other stationary object, it is not a collision. The second fault lies in the expression 'in collision with'. Many writers, anxious not to impute blame in articles dealing with accidents, resort to this awkward phrase, but generally unnecessarily. Clearly some care must be taken not to appear to place blame on one party when the person at fault is not known, but saying 'the two cars collided' is actually safer and more neutral than writing that one was 'in collision with' another.

collision. See COLLIDE, COLLISION.

collusion. 'They have been working in collusion on the experiments for almost four years' (*Guardian*). Let us hope, for the sake of the *Guardian*, that they read another newspaper that day, for *collusion* means to work together for ends that are fraudulent or underhanded. In the example above, describing the work of two scientists, the word wanted was 'cooperation' or 'collaboration'.

Colombia is the name of the South American country and it is misspelled shamefully often: 'The book has now been turned into a television series in Columbia' (*Sunday Times*); 'The programme looks at coffee in Columbia and the problems of land ownership . . .' (*Daily Mail*). The problem arises because the man known in his native Italy as Cristoforo Colombo became in English Christopher Columbus. Thus words derived from his name in English – Columbia University, the District of Columbia, British Columbia – carry a 'u', but those originated by speakers of Romance languages are spelled with an 'o' in the second syllable.

Colosseum. See COLISEUM, COLOSSEUM.

comic, comical. 'There was a comic side to the tragedy' (*The Times*). Something that is comic is intended to be funny. Something that is comical is funny whether or not that was the intention. Since tragedies are never intentionally amusing, the word wanted here was *comical*.

comical. See COMIC, COMICAL.

commence. 'Work on the project is scheduled to commence in June' (*Financial Times*). An unnecessary genteelism. What's wrong with 'begin'?

common. See MUTUAL, COMMON.

comparatively. 'Comparatively little progress was made in the talks yesterday' (*Guardian*). Compared with what? *Comparatively* should be reserved for occasions when a comparison is being expressed or at least clearly implied. If all you mean is 'fairly' or 'only', choose another word. (See also RELATIVELY.)

compare to, compare with. These two can be usefully distinguished. *Compare to* should be used to liken things, *compare with* to consider their similarities or differences. 'He compared London to New York' means that he felt London to be similar to New York. 'He compared London with New York' means that he assessed the two cities' relative merits. *Compare to* most often appears in figurative senses, as in 'Shall I compare thee to a summer's day?' So unless you are writing poetry or love letters, *compare with* is usually the expression you want.

A separate problem sometimes arises when writers try to compare incomparables. Fowler cites this example: 'Dryden's prose . . . loses nothing of its value by being compared with his contemporaries'. The writer has inadvertently compared prose with people when he meant to compare prose with prose. It should be 'with that of his contemporaries'.

compatriot for a fellow countryman. Not to be confused, in meaning or spelling, with *expatriate*, for someone who has taken up residence in a new land.

compel, impel. Both words imply the application of a force leading to some form of action, but they are not quite synonymous. *Compel* is the stronger of the two and, like its cousin *compulsion*, suggests action undertaken as a result of coercion or irresistible pressure: 'The man's bullying tactics compelled me to step forward'. *Impel* is closer in meaning to 'encourage' and means to urge forward: 'The audience's ovation impelled me to speak at greater length than I had intended'. If you are compelled to do something, you have no choice. If you are impelled, an element of willingness is possible.

compendium. No doubt because of the similarity in sound to 'comprehensive', the word is often taken to mean vast and all-embracing. In fact, a compendium is a succinct summary or abridgement. Size has nothing to do with it. It may be as large as *The Oxford English Dictionary* or as small as a memorandum. What is important is that it should provide a complete summary in a brief way. The plural can be either *compendia* or *compendiums*. The *OED* prefers the former, most other dictionaries the latter.

complacent, complaisant. The first means self-satisfied, contented to the point of smugness. The second means affable and cheerfully obliging. If you are complacent, you are pleased with yourself. If you are complaisant, you wish to please others. Both words come from the Latin *complacere* ('to please'), but *complaisant* reached us by way of France, which accounts for the difference in spelling.

complaisant. See COMPLACENT, COMPLAISANT.

complement, compliment. The words come from the same Latin root, *complere*, meaning to fill up, but have long had separate meanings. *Compliment* means to praise. *Complement* has stayed closer to the original meaning: to fill out or make whole. As such, it should have been used here: 'To compliment the shopping there will also be a large leisure content including a ten-screen cinema, nightclub, disco and entertainments complex' (advertisement in the *Financial Times*).

complete. Partridge includes *complete* in his list of false comparatives – that is, words that do not admit of comparison, such as 'ultimate' and 'eternal' (one thing cannot be 'more ultimate' or 'more eternal' than another). Technically, he is right, and you should take care not to modify *complete* needlessly. But there are occasions when it would be pedantic to carry the stricture too far. As the Morrises note, there can be no real objection to 'This is the most complete study to date of that period'. Use it, but use it judiciously.

compliment. See COMPLEMENT, COMPLIMENT.

compound. 'News of a crop failure in the northern part of the country will only compound the government's economic and political problems' (*The Times*). Several authorities have deplored the use of *compound* in the sense of worsen, as it is employed above and increasingly elsewhere. They are right to point out that the usage springs from a misinterpretation of the word's original and more narrow meanings, though that in itself is insufficient cause to shirk it. Many other words have arrived at their present meanings through misinterpretation; see, for instance, INTERNECINE.

A more pertinent consideration is whether we need *compound* in its looser sense. The answer must be no. In the example above, the writer might have used instead 'multiply', 'aggravate', 'heighten', 'worsen', 'exacerbate', 'add to', 'intensify' or any of a dozen other words.

We should also remember that *compound* is already a busy word. Dictionaries list up to nine distinct meanings for it as a verb, seven as a noun and nine as an adjective. In some of these, the word's meanings are narrow. In legal parlance, for instance, *compound* has the very specific meaning of to forgo prosecution in return for payment or some other consideration (it is from this that we get the widely misunderstood phrase 'to compound a felony', which has nothing to do with aggravation). To use *compound* in the sense of worsen in such a context is bound to be misleading.

All that said, most dictionaries recognize the newer meaning, so it cannot be called incorrect, but you should be aware that some more conservative users of English may object to it and with some grounds.

comprise. 'He is the first director with the nerve to capitalize on something very obvious: audiences are comprised of ordinary people' (*Observer*). They are not. Audiences are *composed* of ordinary people. *Comprised of* is a common expression, but it is always wrong. *Comprise* means to contain. The whole comprises the parts and not vice versa. A house may comprise seven rooms, but seven rooms do not comprise a house – and still less is a house comprised of seven rooms. The error is seen again here: 'Beneath Sequoia is the Bechtel Group, a holding company comprised of three main operating arms . . .' (*The New York Times*). It should be either 'a holding company comprising three main operating arms' or 'composed of three main operating arms'.

conceived. 'Last week, 25 years after it was first conceived . . .' (*Time* magazine). Delete 'first'. Something can be conceived only once. Similarly with 'initially conceived' and 'originally conceived'.

concrete. See CEMENT, CONCRETE.

condone. The word does not mean to approve or endorse, senses that are often attached to it. It means to pardon, forgive, overlook. You can condone an action without supporting it.

confectionery. Not *-ary*.

confidant (masc.)/**confidante** (fem.) for a person entrusted with private information.

confidante. See CONFIDANT/CONFIDANTE.

Congo, confusingly, now applies to two neighbouring nations in Africa. The larger of the two, which was called Zaïre until 1977, now styles itself the Democratic Republic of Congo. Bordering it to the west is the much smaller Republic of Congo.

consensus. 'The general consensus in Washington . . .' (*Chicago Tribune*). A tautology. Any consensus must be general. Equally to be avoided is 'consensus of opinion'. Finally, note that *consensus* is spelled with a middle 's', like 'consent'. It has nothing to do with 'census'.

consummate. As a term of praise, the word is much too freely used. A consummate actor is not merely a very good one, but someone who is so good as to be unrivalled or nearly so. It should be reserved to describe only the very best.

contagious, infectious. Diseases spread by contact are contagious. Those spread by air and water are infectious. Used figuratively ('contagious laughter', 'infectious enthusiasm'), either is all right.

contemptible, contemptuous. *Contemptible* means deserving contempt. *Contemptuous* means to bestow it. A contemptible offer may receive a contemptuous response.

contemptuous. See CONTEMPTIBLE, CONTEMPTUOUS.

conterminous, coterminous. The two words mean the same thing, though the first is more commonly used than the second. Both mean to share a boundary.

continual, continuous. Although the distinction is not widely observed, or indeed always necessary, there is a useful difference between the two words. *Continual* refers to things that happen repeatedly but not constantly. *Continuous* indicates an uninterrupted sequence. However, few readers will be aware of this distinction, and the writer who requires absolute clarity will generally be better advised to use 'incessant' or 'uninterrupted' for *continuous* and 'intermittent' for *continual*.

continuous. See CONTINUAL, CONTINUOUS.

contractions. See ABBREVIATIONS, CONTRACTIONS, ACRONYMS.

contrary, converse, opposite, reverse. All four are variously confused at times, which is understandable since their distinctions tend to blur. Briefly, *contrary* describes something that contradicts a proposition. *Converse* applies when the elements of a proposition are reversed. *Opposite* is something that is diametrically opposed to a proposition. *Reverse* can describe any of these.

Take the statement 'I love you'. Its opposite is 'I hate you'. Its converse is 'You love me'. Its contrary would be anything that contradicted it: 'I do not love you', 'I have no feelings at all for you', 'I like you moderately'. The reverse could embrace all of these meanings.

conurbation does not describe any urban area, but rather a place where two or more sizeable communities have sprawled together, such as Pasadena–Los Angeles–Long Beach in California or Leeds–Bradford in England.

converse. See CONTRARY, CONVERSE, OPPOSITE, REVERSE.

convince, persuade. Although often used interchangeably, the words are not quite the same. Briefly, you convince someone that he should believe, but persuade him to act. It is possible to persuade a person to do something without convincing him of the correctness or necessity of doing it. Another distinction is that *persuade* may be followed by an infinitive, but *convince* may not. Thus the following is wrong: 'The Soviet Union evidently is not able to convince Cairo to accept a rapid cease-fire' (*The New York Times*). Make it either 'persuade Cairo to accept' or 'convince Cairo that it should accept'.

cord. See CHORD, CORD.

country, nation. It is perhaps a little fussy to insist too strenuously on the distinction, but, strictly, *country* refers to the geographical characteristics of a place and *nation* to the political and social ones. Thus the United States is one of the richest nations, but largest countries.

Court of St James's is the standard designation of the place to which ambassadors are posted in Great Britain. The absence of an apostrophe and a second 's' is common but wrong, as here: 'He was ambassador to the Court of St James in 1939, when Britain offered him its sword to defend Poland' (*Observer*). St James's also applies as the spelling for the London park and square.

crass means stupid and grossly ignorant to the point of insensitivity and not merely coarse or tasteless. A thing must be pretty bad to be crass.

creole, pidgin. A pidgin – the word is thought to come from a Chinese pronunciation of the English 'business' – is a simplified and rudimentary language that springs up when two or more cultures come in contact. If that contact is prolonged and generations are born for whom the pidgin is their first tongue, the language will usually evolve into a more formalized creole (from the French for 'indigenous'). Most languages that are commonly referred to as pidgins are in fact creoles.

crescendo. 'David English, whose career seemed to be reaching a crescendo this month when he took over editorship of the stumbling Mail on Sunday . . .' (*Sunday Times*). *Crescendo* does not mean reaching a pinnacle, as was apparently intended in the quotation, or signify a loud or explosive conclusion, as it is more commonly misused. Properly, it should be used only to describe a gradual increase in volume or intensity.

criteria, criterion. 'The sole criteria now is personal merit, an immigration official said' (*Independent*). He should have said *criterion*. Remember: one criterion, two criteria.

criterion. See CRITERIA, CRITERION.

Crome Yellow for the 1921 novel by Aldous Huxley. Not *Chrome*.

cross-Channel ferry is, in most contexts, a tautology. It is enough to call it a Channel ferry.

culminate. 'The company's financial troubles culminated in the resignation of the chairman last June' (*The Times*). *Culminate* does not signify any result or outcome, but rather one marking a high point. A series of battles may culminate in a final victory, but financial troubles do not culminate in a resignation.

current, currently. When there is a need to contrast the present with the past, *current* has its place, but all too often it is merely an idle occupier of space, as in these two examples from a single article in *Time* magazine: 'The Government currently owns 740 million acres, or 32.7% of the land in the U.S.'; 'Property in the area is currently fetching $125 to $225 per acre'. The notion of currency is implicit in both statements, as it is in most other sentences in which *current* and *currently* appear. *Currently* should be deleted from both. (The second sentence could be further improved by changing 'is fetching' to 'fetches'.)

currently. See CURRENT, CURRENTLY.

curricula vitae is the plural of curriculum vitae.

curtsy. Not *-ey*.

curvaceous. Not *-ious*.

cut back. 'Losses in the metal stamping division have forced the group to cut back production' (*Daily Telegraph*). More succinct to say 'have forced the group to cut production'. The noun form *cutback* is often similarly pleonastic. 'Spending cutbacks' can almost always be shortened to 'spending cuts'. (See PHRASAL VERBS.)

D

dais. See LECTERN, PODIUM, DAIS, ROSTRUM.

dangling modifiers are one of the more complicated and disagreeable aspects of English usage, but at least they provide some compensation by being frequently amusing. Every authority has a stock of illustrative howlers. Fowler, for instance, gives us 'Handing me my whisky, his face broke into an awkward smile' (that rare thing, a face that can pass whisky), while Bernstein offers 'Although sixty-one years old when he wore the original suit, his waist was only thirty-five' and 'When dipped in melted butter or Hollandaise sauce, one truly deserves the food of the gods'.

Most often, dangling modifiers are caused by unattached present participles. But they can also involve past and perfect participles, appositive phrases, clauses, infinitives or simple adjectives.* Occasionally the element to be modified is missing altogether: 'As reconstructed by the police, Pfeffer at first denied any knowledge of the Byrd murder' (cited by Bernstein). It was not, of course, Pfeffer that was reconstructed by the police, but the facts or story or some other noun that is only implied.

Regardless of the part of speech at fault, there is in every dangling modifier a failure by the writer to say what he means because of a simple mispositioning of words. Consider this example: 'Slim, of medium height and with sharp features, Mr Smith's technical skills are combined with strong leadership qual-

---

* Strictly speaking, only adverbs modify; nouns and adjectives qualify. But because the usage problems are essentially the same for all the parts of speech, I have collected them under the heading by which they are most commonly, if not quite accurately, known.

ities' (*The New York Times*). As written, the sentence is telling us that Mr Smith's technical skills are slim and of medium height. It needs to be recast as 'Slim, of medium height and with sharp features, he combines technical skills with strong leadership qualities' or words to that effect (but see NON SEQUITUR).

Or consider this sentence from *Time* magazine: 'In addition to being cheap and easily obtainable, Crotti claims that the bags have several advantages over other methods'. We can reasonably assume that it is not Crotti that is cheap and easily obtainable, but the bags. Again, recasting is needed: 'In addition to being cheap and easily obtainable, the bags have several advantages over other methods, Crotti claims' (but see CLAIM).

William and Mary Morris offer a simple remedy to the problem of dangling modifiers – namely that after having written the modifying phrase or clause, you should make sure that the next word is the one to which the modifier pertains. That is sound enough advice, but, like so much else in English usage, it will take you only so far.

There are, to begin with, a number of participial phrases that have the effect of prepositions or conjunctions, and you may dangle them as you will without breaking any rules. They include *generally speaking, concerning, regarding, judging, owing to, failing, speaking of* and many others. There are also certain stock phrases and idiomatic constructions that flout the rule but are still acceptable, such as 'putting two and two together' and 'getting down to brass tacks'.

It is this multiplicity of exceptions that makes the subject so difficult. If I write, 'As the author of this book, let me say this', am I perpetrating a dangling modifier or simply resorting to idiom? It depends very much on which authority you consult.

It is perhaps also worth noting that opprobrium for the dangling modifier is not universal. The Evanses, after asserting that the problem has been common among good writers at least since Chaucer, call the rule banning its use 'pernicious' and add that 'no one who takes it as inviolable can write good English'. They maintain that the problem with sentences such as 'Handing me my whisky, his face broke into a broad grin' is not that the participle is dangling, but rather that it isn't. It sounds absurd only because 'his face' is so firmly attached to the participial phrase. But when a note of absurdity is not sounded, they say, the sentence should be allowed to pass.

They are certainly right to caution against becoming obsessed with dangling modifiers, but there is, I think, a clearer need than they allow to watch out for them. Certainly if you find yourself writing a phrase that permits the merest hint of incongruity, it is time to recast your sentence.

danke schön is the correct spelling for 'thank you very much' in German.

danse macabre, not *dance*, from the French for 'a dance of death'. The plural is *danses macabres*.

data. Perhaps no other word better illustrates the extent to which English usage is often largely a matter of fashion. In Latin, *data* is of course a plural, and until fairly recent times virtually all authorities insisted, often quite strenuously, that it be treated as such in English. Thus 'The data was fed into a computer program known as SLOSH' (*New Yorker*) should be 'The data were fed . . .'.

The problem is that etymology doesn't always count for much in English. If it did, we would have to write, 'My stamina aren't what they used to be' or 'I've just paid two insurance premia'. The fact is, of course, that for centuries we have been adapting Latin words to fit the needs and patterns of English. 'Museums', 'agendas', 'stadiums', 'premiums' and many others are freely, and unexceptionably, inflected on the English model, not the Latin one.

There is an increasing tendency among many users of English to treat all Latin plurals as singulars, even those that have tradition-ally been treated as plural, most notably 'criteria', 'media', 'phenomena', 'strata' and *data*. With the first four of these the impulse is better resisted, partly as a concession to convention, but also because there is a clear and useful distinction to be made between the singular and plural forms. In stratified rock, for instance, each stratum is clearly delineated. In any list of criteria, each criterion is distinguishable from every other. Media suggests – or ought to suggest – one medium and another medium and another. In each case the elements that make up the whole are invariably distinct and separable.

But with *data* such distinctions are much less evident. This may be because, as Quirk has suggested, we have a natural inclination to regard *data* as an aggregate – that is, as a word in which we perceive the whole more immediately than the parts. Just as we see a bowlful of sugar as a distinct entity rather than as a collection of granules (which is why we don't say, 'Sugar are sweet'), so we tend to see *data* as a complete whole rather than one datum and another datum and another. In this regard it is similar to 'news' (which some nineteenth-century users actually treated as plural) or 'information'.

The shift is clearly in the direction of treating *data* as a singular, as the *New Yorker* and several other publications have decided to do. Personally, and no doubt perversely, I find that I have grown more attached to *data* as a plural with the passage of time. I think there is a certain elegance and precision in 'More data are needed to provide a fuller picture of the DNA markers' (*Nature*) than 'The data by itself is vacuous' (*The New York Times*). But that is of course no more than my opinion.

Whichever side you come down on, it is worth observing that the sense of *data* is generally best confined to the idea of raw, uncollated bits of information, the sort of stuff churned out by computers, and not used as a simple synonym for facts or reports or information, as it was in this *New York Times* headline: 'Austria Magazine Reports New Data on Waldheim and Nazis'. The 'data', on inspection, proved to be evidence and allegations – words that would have more comfortably fitted the context, if not the headline space.

dates. Many writers have a tendency to put commas into dates where they are required by neither sense nor convention. Consider these three examples: 'The storm was the worst since January, 1947' (*Observer*); 'He was arrested on 12 November, 1985' (*Independent*); 'Cribbins was born on December 8, 1952, in Sarasota, Florida' (*The New York Times*). Only the last example is correctly punctuated. The reason for putting the comma between the date and year is simply to separate the two numbers to avoid any possibility of confusion. But where the style of a publication is to interpose the month between the two dates (as with '12 November 1985'), there is no need to add a separating comma; the name of the month does that already. Similarly, when there are not two numbers to separate, as in the first example, a separating comma is superfluous. Incidentally, note the comma after 1952 in the *New York Times* example. Logically it is unnecessary, but the convention is to include it. Similarly if the sentence were lengthened, it would be conventional to put a comma after Florida.

A separate common failing with dates is seen here: 'The by-election date will be announced on March 10th' (*Guardian*). Delete the 'th'. It isn't necessary. (See also YEAR.)

dB is the abbreviation for decibel.

decimate. Literally the word means to reduce by a tenth (from the ancient practice of punishing the mutinous or cowardly by killing every tenth man). By extension it may be used to describe the inflicting of heavy damage, but it should never be used to denote annihilation, as in this memorably excruciating sentence cited by Fowler: 'Dick, hotly pursued by the scalp-hunter, turned in his saddle, fired and literally decimated his opponent'. Equally to be avoided are contexts in which the word's use is clearly inconsistent with its literal meaning, as in 'Frost decimated an estimated 80 per cent of the crops'.

defective, deficient. When something is not working properly, it is defective; when it is missing a necessary part, it is deficient.

deficient. See DEFECTIVE, DEFICIENT.

definite, definitive. *Definite* means precise and unmistakable. *Definitive* means final and conclusive. A definite offer is a clear one; a definitive offer is one that permits of no haggling.

definitive. See DEFINITE, DEFINITIVE.

defuse, diffuse. Occasionally confused, as here: 'In an attempt to diffuse panic over the disease, he spelled out the ways in which it was spread' (*Independent*). The 'he' above refers to the Archbishop of Canterbury, who is hardly likely to wish to scatter panic, however thinly. That is the meaning of *diffuse*: to disperse or disseminate, to take a given volume and distribute it more widely. The notion of making less harmful is contained in the word *defuse*, which is of course the sense that the writer intended.

delectable. Not *-ible*.

demean. Some authorities, among them Fowler, object to the word in the sense of to debase or degrade, pointing out that its original, more neutral meaning signified only conduct or behaviour (a neutrality preserved in the cognate form *demeanour*). But, as Bernstein notes, the looser usage has been with us since 1601, which suggests that it may be just a bit late to try to hold the line now.

demise. 'But fears about the demise of the US economy look exaggerated' (*Observer*). They would just about have to. *Demise* does not mean decline, as is all too often thought. It means death. It applies to things that no longer exist at all.

deplete, reduce. Though their meanings are roughly the same, *deplete* has the additional connotation of injurious reduction. As the Evanses note, a garrison may be reduced by administrative order, but depleted by sickness.

deplore. Strictly, you may deplore a thing, but not a person. I may deplore your behaviour, but I cannot deplore you.

deprecate. '. . . but he deprecated the significance of his achievement' (*Los Angeles Times*). *Deprecate* does not mean to play down or show modesty, as is often intended. It means to disapprove of strongly or to protest against. Although not always supported by dictionaries now, the distinction is still widely observed, and should at least be familiar to any professional user of English.

de rigueur. Often misspelled, as here: 'A few decades ago, when dinner jackets were de rigeur . . .' (*Daily Telegraph*). Note that it has two 'u's.

derisive, derisory. Something that is derisive conveys ridicule or contempt. Something that is derisory invites it. A derisory offer is likely to provoke a derisive response.

derisory. See DERISIVE, DERISORY.

despite, in spite of. There is no distinction between the two. A common construction is seen here: 'But despite the fall in sterling, Downing Street officials were at pains to play down any suggestion of crisis' (*Daily Telegraph*). Because *despite* and *in spite of* indicate a change of emphasis, 'but' is generally superfluous with either. It is enough to say: 'Despite the fall in sterling, Downing Street officials . . .'.

destroy is an incomparable – almost. If a house is consumed by fire, it is enough to say that it was destroyed, not that it was 'completely destroyed' or 'totally destroyed'. However, and illogical as it may seem, it is all right to speak of a house that has been partly destroyed. There is simply no other way of putting it without resorting to more circuitous descriptions. That is perhaps absurd and inconsistent, but ever thus was English.

diagnosis, prognosis. To make a diagnosis is to identify and define a problem, usually a disease. A prognosis is a projection of the course and likely outcome of a problem. *Diagnosis* applies only to conditions, not to people. Thus 'Asbestos victims were not diagnosed in large numbers until the 1960s' (*Time* magazine) is not quite right. It was the victims' conditions that were not diagnosed, not the victims themselves.

dialect, patois. Both describe the form of language prevailing in a region and can be used interchangeably, though *patois* is normally better reserved for contexts involving French or its variants. 'He spoke in the patois of Yorkshire' is at best jocular. The plural of *patois*, incidentally, is also *patois*.

differ, diverge. 'There now seems some hope that these divergent views can be reconciled' (*Daily Telegraph*). Strictly speaking, that is unlikely. When two things diverge, they move further apart (just as when they converge they come together). It is not a word that should be applied freely to any difference of opinion, but only to those in which a rift is widening.

different. Often used unnecessarily. 'He plays milkmaid to more than 50 different species of poisonous snake' (*Observer*); 'The phenomenally successful Rubik Cube, which has 43,252,002,274,489,856,000 different permutations but only one solution' (*Sunday Times*); '[He] published at least five different books on grammar' (Simon, *Paradigms Lost*). Frequently, as in each of these examples, it can be deleted without loss.

different from, to, than. Among the more tenacious beliefs of some writers and editors is that *different* may be followed only by *from*. At least since 1906, when the Fowler brothers raised the issue in *The King's English*, authorities have pointed out that there is no real basis for this belief, but still it persists.

Different from is, to be sure, the usual form in most sentences and the only acceptable form in some, as when it precedes a noun or pronoun ('My car is different from his'; 'Men are different from women'). But when *different* introduces a clause, there can be no valid objection to following it with a *to* (though this usage is chiefly British) or *than*, as in this sentence by John Maynard Keynes: 'How different things appear in Washington than in London'. You may, if you insist, change it to 'How different things appear in Washington from how they appear in London', but all it gives you is more words, not better grammar.

diffuse. See DEFUSE, DIFFUSE.

dilemma. 'The chief dilemma facing Mr Greenspan is whether or not to raise interest rates' (*Sunday Times*). *Dilemma* does not mean just any difficulty or predicament. Strictly speaking, it applies only when someone is faced with two courses of action, both unsatisfactory. Fowler accepted its extension to contexts involving more than two alternatives, but even then the number of alternatives should be definite and the consequences of each unappealing.

DiMaggio, Joe, for the American baseball player and husband of Marilyn Monroe.

diphtheria. Note that the first syllable is spelled *diph-*, not *dipth-*, and is pronounced accordingly.

disassemble, dissemble. 'It would almost have been cheaper to dissemble the factory and move it to Wales' (*Sunday Times*). Actually, no. Unlike 'dissociate' and 'disassociate', which mean the same thing, *dissemble* and *disassemble* have quite separate meanings. *Dissemble* means to conceal. If someone close to you dies, you may dissemble your grief with a smile. The word wanted in the example above was *disassemble*, which means to take apart.

disassociate, dissociate. The first is not incorrect, but the second has the virtue of brevity.

discernible. Not *-able*.

discomfit, discomfort. 'In this she is greatly assisted by her husband . . . who enjoys spreading discomfiture in a good cause as much as she does' (*Observer*). The writer here, like many before him, clearly meant *discomfort*, which has nothing in common with *discomfiture* beyond a superficial resemblance. *Discomfit* means to rout, overwhelm or completely disconcert. Some dictionaries, particularly in America, now accept the newer sense of to perplex or induce uneasiness, but I would submit that the distinction is very much worth preserving. If *discomfort* is the condition you have in mind, why not use that word and leave *discomfiture* for less discriminating users?

discomfort. See DISCOMFIT, DISCOMFORT.

discreet, discrete. The first means circumspect, careful, showing good judgement ('He promised to be discreet in his inquiries'). The second means unattached or unrelated ('The compound was composed of discrete particles').

discrete. See DISCREET, DISCRETE.

disinterested, uninterested. 'Gerulaitis, after appearing almost disinterested in the first set, took a 5–1 lead in the second' (*The New York Times*). A participant in a tennis match might appear uninterested, but he would be unlikely to be disinterested, which means neutral and impartial. A disinterested person is one who has no stake in the outcome of an event; an uninterested person is one who doesn't care. As with DISCOMFIT and DISCOMFORT (see above), the distinction is a useful one and well worth fighting for.

disorientated. Use it if you will, but *disoriented* is shorter.

dispensable. Not *-ible*.

disposal, disposition. If you are talking about getting rid of, use *disposal* ('the disposal of nuclear weapons'). If you mean arranging, use *disposition* ('the disposition of troops on the battlefield').

disposition. See DISPOSAL, DISPOSITION.

dissemble. See DISASSEMBLE, DISSEMBLE.

dissociate. See DISASSOCIATE, DISSOCIATE.

distrait, distraught. The first means abstracted in thought, absent-minded. The second means deeply agitated.

distraught. See DISTRAIT, DISTRAUGHT.

disturb, perturb. They can often be used interchangeably, but generally the first is better applied to physical agitation, the second to mental agitation.

diverge. See DIFFER, DIVERGE.

Dobermann pinscher for the breed of dog. The American spelling is Doberman pinscher.

Dormobile for the type of vehicle. The name is a trade mark so it should be used only for vehicles of that name and not generically.

dormouse for the small rodent, which isn't actually a mouse at all. The name is thought to be a corruption of the Norman French *dormeus*, meaning sleepy. The plural is *dormice*.

dos and don'ts. Not *do's*.

double meanings. 'Oil slick talks' (*Times* headline). Now that is news. Anyone who has written headlines for a living will know the deep embarrassment that comes from causing vast hilarity to a large group of people by writing an inadvertently two-faced headline. I have no doubt that someone at the *Toronto Globe and Mail* is still cringing at having written 'Upturns May Indicate Some Bottoms Touched' (cited in *Punch*), as must earlier have been the author of the oft-quoted and variously attributed 'McArthur flies back to front'. It is always worth remembering that many words carry a range of meanings, or function as both nouns and verbs, and consequently offer unexpected opportunities for mischief. 'Talks', as in the opening citation, is particularly susceptible to two interpretations. The result may not always be hilarious, but it is frequently a touch absurd, as with the following, all culled from the *Times* briefs columns over a period of about six weeks: 'China talks', 'Rubber talks', 'Tin talks', 'Job talks', 'School talks'.

double negatives. Most people know that you shouldn't say, 'I haven't had no dinner', but some writers, doubtless more out of haste than ignorance, sometimes perpetrate sentences that are scarcely less jarring, as here: 'Stranded and uncertain of their location, the survivors endured for six days without hardly a trace of food' (*Chicago Tribune*). Since 'hardly', like 'scarcely', has the grammatical effect of a negative, it requires no further negation. Make it 'with hardly'.

Some usage guides flatly condemn all double negatives, but there is one kind – in which a negative in the main clause is paralleled in a subordinate construction – that we might view more tolerantly. The Evanses cite this sentence from Jane Austen: 'There was none too poor or remote not to feel an interest'. And Shakespeare wrote: 'Nor what he said, though it lacked form a little, was not like madness'. But such constructions must be considered exceptional. More often the intrusion of a second negative is merely a sign of fuzzy writing. At best it will force the reader to pause and perform some verbal arithmetic, adding negative to negative, as here: 'The plan is now thought unlikely not to go ahead' (*The Times*). At worst it may leave the reader darkly baffled, as in this memorably convoluted sentence from a leading authority: 'Moreover . . . our sense of linguistic tact will not urge us not to use words that may offend or irritate' (Quirk, *The Use of English*).

doubt if, that, whether. Idiom demands some selectivity in the choice of conjunction to introduce a clause after *doubt* and *doubtful*. The rule is simple: *doubt that* should be reserved for negative contexts ('There is no doubt that . . .'; 'It was never doubtful that . . .') and interrogative ones ('Do you have any doubt that . . . ?'; 'Was it ever doubtful that . . . ?'). *Whether* or *if* should be used in all others ('I doubt if he will come'; 'It is doubtful whether the rain will stop').

doubtless, undoubtedly, indubitably. 'Tonight he faces what is doubtlessly the toughest and loneliest choice of his 13-year stewardship of the Palestine Liberation Organization' (*Washington Post*). Since *doubtless* can be an adverb as well as an adjective, there is no need to add -*ly* to it. *Undoubtedly* would have been a better choice still because, as the Evanses note, it has a less concessive air. *Doubtless* usually suggests a tone of reluctance or resignation: 'You are doubtless right'. *Undoubtedly* carries more conviction: 'You are undoubtedly right'. *Indubitably* is a somewhat jocular synonym for either.

douse, dowse. The first means to drench; the second means to search for water.

dowse. See DOUSE, DOWSE.

drunken driving. Not *drunk driving*.

drunkenness. Misspelled much too often, as here: 'Drunkeness, particularly behind the wheel of a car, has not been a serious problem in Italy' (*Independent*). Note -*nn*-.

due to. Most authorities continue to accept that *due* is an adjective only and must always modify a noun. Thus 'He was absent due to illness' would be wrong. We could correct it either by writing 'He was absent because of [or owing to] illness' or by recasting the sentence in such a way as to give *due* a noun to modify, e.g., 'His absence was due to illness'.

The rule is mystifyingly inconsistent – no one has ever really explained why 'owing to' used prepositionally is acceptable, while *due to* used prepositionally is not – but it should perhaps still be observed, at least in formal writing, if only to avoid a charge of ignorance.

E

each is not always an easy word, even for the authorities. Here are William and Mary Morris writing in *The Harper Dictionary of Contemporary Usage*: 'Each of the variants indicated in boldface type count as an entry'. Make it 'counts'. As the Morrises doubtless knew but failed to note, when *each* is the subject of a sentence the verb should be singular.

However, a plural verb is correct when the sentence has another subject and *each* is a mere adjunct. Again, we can cite an error made by an authority, in this case Philip Howard in *The State of the Language*: 'The separate genres of journalism each creates its own jargon, as any specialized subject or activity always does'. It should be 'each create their own jargon'. 'Genres' is the subject of that sentence, so the verb must respond to it.

Deciding whether to use a singular or plural verb is not as difficult as it may at first seem. In fact, the rule could hardly be more straightforward. When *each* precedes the noun or pronoun to which it refers, the verb should be singular: 'Each of us was . . .'. When it follows the noun or pronoun, the verb should be plural: 'We each were . . .'.

Each not only influences the number of the verb, it also influences the number of later nouns and pronouns. In simpler terms, if *each* precedes the verb, subsequent nouns and pronouns should be plural (e.g., 'They each are subject to sentences of five years'), but if *each* follows the verb, the subsequent nouns and pronouns should be singular ('They are each subject to a sentence of five years').

each and every is at best a trite way of providing emphasis, at worst redundant, and generally both, as here: 'Each and every one of the 12 songs on Marshall Crenshaw's debut album is breezy and refreshing' (*Washington Post*). Equally to be avoided is *each individual*, as in 'Players do not have to face the perils of qualifying for each individual tournament' (*The New York Times*). In both cases *each* alone would have been sufficient.

each other, one another. A few arbiters of usage continue to insist on *each other* for two things and *one another* for more than two. There is no harm in observing such a distinction, but also little to be gained from it, and, as Fowler long ago noted, the practice has no basis in historical usage.

Earhart, Amelia, for the American aviator who famously disappeared while trying to circumnavigate the globe in 1937.

Earth, earth. When considering it as a planet, particularly in apposition to other cosmic features, *Earth* should be capitalized. In other senses, it should be lower case.

economic, economical. If what you mean is cheap and thrifty, use *economical*. For every other sense use *economic*. An economic rent is one that is not too cheap for the landlord. An economical rent is one that is not too expensive for the tenant.

economical. See ECONOMIC, ECONOMICAL.

Ecuadorean is generally the preferred spelling for a person or product from Ecuador.

effect. See AFFECT, EFFECT.

effete. 'Nor is it a concern only to the highly educated, or the effete Northeast, or to city folk' (Newman, *A Civil Tongue*). *Effete* does not mean affectedly intellectual or sophisticated, as was apparently intended here, or effeminate and weak, as it is more often used elsewhere. It means exhausted and barren. An effete poet is not necessarily intellectual or foppish, but rather someone whose creative impulses are spent.

e.g., i.e. The first is an abbreviation of *exempli gratia* and means 'for example', as in 'Some words are homonyms, e.g., blew and blue'. The second is the abbreviation for *id est* and means 'that is' or 'that is to say', as in 'He is pusillanimous, i.e., lacking in courage'.

egoism, egotism. The first pertains to the philosophical notion that a person can prove nothing beyond the existence of his own mind. It is the opposite of altruism and is better left to contexts involving metaphysics and ethics. If all you wish to suggest is inflated vanity or preoccupation with the self, use *egotism*.

egotism. See EGOISM, EGOTISM.

Eiffel Tower, Paris, but *Eifel Mountains*, Germany.

eisteddfod is the correct spelling for a Welsh festival or competition of music or literature. The plural is *eisteddfods* or (in Welsh) *eisteddfodau*.

either. 'Decisions on Mansfield's economy are now made in either Detroit, Pittsburgh or New York' (*The New York Times*). *Either* suggests a duality and is almost always better avoided when the context involves quantities of more than two. Often in such constructions, as in the example cited, it is a clumsy intrusion; delete it and the sentence says no less. A separate problem with *either* is seen here: 'But in every case the facts either proved too elusive or the explanations too arcane to be satisfactory'. *Either* should be placed before 'the facts' or deleted; for a discussion, see BOTH ... AND. For a discussion of errors of number involving *either*, see NEITHER.

eke. 'After a series of fits and starts yesterday the stock market eked out a gain' (cited by Bernstein). *Eke* means to add to or supplement in a meagre way. It does not mean to squeeze out, as was intended in the example above. You eke out an original supply – either by adding to it or by consuming it frugally – but you do not eke out a result.

elegy, eulogy. The first is a mournful poem; the second is a tribute to the dead.

elemental, elementary. *Elemental* refers to things that are basic or primary: 'Physiology is an elemental part of a medical student's studies'. *Elementary* means simple or introductory: 'This phrase book provides an elementary guide to Spanish'.

elementary. See ELEMENTAL, ELEMENTARY.

elicit, extract, extort. These three are broadly synonymous, but are distinguished by the degree of force that they imply. *Elicit*, the mildest of the three, means to draw or coax out, and can additionally suggest an element of craftiness: you can elicit information without the informant being aware that he has divulged it. *Extract* suggests a stronger and more persistent effort, possibly involving threats or importuning. *Extort* is stronger still and suggests clear threats of violence or harm.

embalmment. Note *-mm-*.

embarrass, embarrassment. Both are quite often misspelled. Note, however, that the French spelling is *embarras*, as in *embarras de richesses* (an embarrassment of riches) and *embarras du choix* (an embarrassment of choice).

embarrassment. See EMBARRASS, EMBARRASSMENT.

Emmental for the cheese.

empathy, sympathy. *Empathy* denotes a close emotional understanding of the feelings or problems of another. It is thus close in meaning to 'compassion'. *Sympathy* is more general. It can denote a closeness of understanding, but it can equally suggest no more than an abstract or intellectual awareness of another's misfortune. *Empathy* generally applies only to serious misfortunes; *sympathy* can apply to any small annoyance or setback.

empower. Not *en-*.

encumbrance. Not *-erance*.

endemic. See EPIDEMIC.

enormity. 'Some people ... lamented that the men whom America sent into space were not articulate or impassioned enough to register the enormity of their undertaking' (*New Yorker*). *Enormity* does not, as is frequently thought, indicate size, but refers to something that is wicked, monstrous and outrageous ('The enormity of Hitler's crimes will never be forgotten'). In the example above, the writer should have said 'enormousness' – or, better still, found a less ungainly synonym like 'immensity' or 'vastness'.

enquiry. See QUERY, INQUIRY, ENQUIRY.

envisage, envision. Both words suggest the calling up of a mental image. *Envision* is slightly the loftier of the two. You might envision a better life for yourself, but if all you are thinking about is how the dining room will look when the walls have been repainted, *envisage* is probably the better word. If no mental image is involved, neither word is correct. A rough rule is that if you find yourself following either word with *that*, you are using it incorrectly, as here: 'He envisaged that there would be no access to the school from the main road' (cited by Gowers).

envision. See ENVISAGE, ENVISION.

epidemic. Strictly speaking, only people can suffer an epidemic (the word means 'in or among people'). An outbreak of disease among animals is epizootic. It is also worth noting that *epidemic* refers only to outbreaks. When a disease or other problem is of long standing, it is endemic.

epigram, epigraph. The first is a short, witty saying or poem. The second is an inscription, as on a monument or statue, or an introductory quotation at the beginning of a book or substantial block of text.

epigraph. See EPIGRAM, EPIGRAPH.

equable, equitable. Most dictionaries define *equable* merely as meaning steady and unvarying, but it should also convey the sense of being remote from extremes. A consistently hot climate is not equable, no matter how unvarying the temperature. Similarly, someone whose outlook is invariably sunny cannot properly be described as having an equable temperament.

Equitable, with which *equable* is sometimes confused, means fair and impartial. An equitable settlement is a just one.

equally as is illiterate. 'This is equally as good' should be 'This is equally good' or 'This is as good'.

Equatorial Guinea. See GUINEA, GUINEA-BISSAU, EQUA-TORIAL GUINEA.

equitable. See EQUABLE, EQUITABLE.

equivocal. See AMBIGUOUS, EQUIVOCAL.

especial. See SPECIAL, ESPECIAL.

especially, specially. 'It is designed to compete with coal, specially in the south where delivery costs tend to make coal more expensive' (*Independent*). Make it *especially* in the south. *Specially* means for a specific purpose or occasion, as in 'a specially designed wedding dress'. *Especially* means particularly, pre-eminently or exceptionally, as in 'an especially talented singer'. A simple guide is to ask yourself whether you could substitute 'particularly'. If so, the word you want is *especially*.

estimated at about. 'The crowd was estimated at about 50,000' (*Los Angeles Times*). Because *estimated* contains the idea of an approximation, *about* is superfluous. Delete it.

et cetera (etc.). 'Thousands competed, thousands watched and thousands also observed – volunteers all of them – who only pinned numbers, massaged muscles, supplied water, charted positions, screamed encouragement, etc.' (*Los Angeles Times*). In lexicography and other types of technical writing, *etc.* has its place. But in newspapers and magazines its use can suggest that the writer didn't know what else he meant or, as in the foregoing example, was too lazy to tell us. Generally it is better avoided.

eulogy. See ELEGY, EULOGY.

evangelical, evangelistic. Generally, *evangelical* is better reserved for contexts pertaining to adherence to the Christian gospel. If you need a word to describe militant zeal or the like, *evangelistic* is almost always better (e.g. 'the evangelistic fervour of the Socialist Alliance').

evangelistic. See EVANGELICAL, EVANGELISTIC.

eventuate. 'Competition for economic interest, power and social esteem can eventuate in community formation only if . . .' (*British Journal of Sociology*, cited by Hudson). A pompous synonym for 'result'.

ever. 'On Wall Street, a late rally provided shares with their largest ever one-day rise' (*The Times*). Many authorities (including the style book of *The Times* itself) object to *ever* in the sense used here on the grounds that the word covers the future as well as the past, and we cannot possibly know what Wall Street shares, or anything else, will be doing tomorrow.

The logic of the argument is impeccable, but it has two short-comings. First, it fails to acknowledge that the usage has been well established for the better part of a century and can thus be defended on grounds of idiom. A more important consideration perhaps is that *ever* often adds a useful air of embracing generality. If I say, 'Have you ever been to Paris?' there is no doubt that I mean at any time in your life. If, however, I say merely, 'Have you been to Paris?' there is some ambiguity as to what span of time we are considering.

In short, there may be a case for using *ever* carefully, even sparingly. But to ban it outright is fussy and unidiomatic and can easily lead to unnecessary confusion.

everybody. See NUMBER(4).

everyone. See NUMBER (4).

exception proves the rule, the. A widely misunderstood expression. As a moment's thought should confirm, it isn't possible for an exception to confirm a rule – but then that isn't the sense that was originally intended. *Prove* here is a 'fossil' – that is, a word or phrase that is now meaningless except within the confines of certain sayings ('hem and haw', 'rank and file' and 'to and fro' are other fossil expressions). Originally *prove* meant 'test' (it comes from the Latin *probo*, 'I test'), so the exception proves the rule meant – and really still ought to mean – that the exception tests the rule. The original meaning of *prove* is preserved more clearly in two other expressions: 'proving ground' and 'the proof of the pudding is in the eating'.

exigent, exiguous. The first means urgent and pressing or exacting and demanding; the second means scanty and slender. But both have a number of synonyms that may spare the reader a trip to the dictionary.

exiguous. See EXIGENT, EXIGUOUS.

exorbitant. Many writers, on both sides of the Atlantic, show a perplexing impulse to put an 'h' into the word, as here: 'This is on the argument that they are troubled by exhorbitant interest charges' (*The Times*). Inhexcusable.

expatriate. Still all too often misspelled, as here: 'Kirov and other Russian expatriots . . .' (*Daily Mail*). Not to be confused with *compatriot*.

expectorate, spit. The distinction between these two is not, it must be conceded, often a matter of great moment, but still it is worth noting that there is a distinction. To spit means to expel saliva; to expectorate is to dredge up and expel phlegm from the lungs. *Expectorate* therefore is not just an unnecessary euphemism for *spit*, it is usually an incorrect one.

expressible. Not *-able*.

extempore, impromptu. Although both words describe unrehearsed remarks or performances, their meanings are slightly different in that *impromptu* can apply only to acts that are improvised at the time of performance, whereas *extempore* suggests only that the actions were undertaken without the benefit of notes or other formal preparation. *Impromptu*, in other words, conveys a greater element of surprise on the part of the speaker or performer.

extort. See ELICIT, EXTRACT, EXTORT.

extract. See ELICIT, EXTRACT, EXTORT.

extraneous. Not *exter-*.

extrovert. Not *extra-*.

eyeing is the correct spelling in the sense of to look something over.

F

fable, parable, allegory, myth. Fables and parables are both stories intended to have instructional value. They differ in that parables are always concerned with religious or ethical themes, while fables are usually concerned with more practical considerations (and frequently have animals as the characters). An allegory is an extended metaphor – that is, a narrative in which the principal characters represent things that are not explicitly stated. Orwell's *Animal Farm* is an allegory. Myths originally were stories designed to explain some belief or phenomenon, usually through the exploits of superhuman beings. Today the word can signify any popular misconception or invented story.

façade. 'Above the pilasters, on the front facade, is a five-story-high keystone . . .' (*Time* magazine). Although most dictionaries allow that *façade* can apply to any side of a building, it normally indicates the front (or face), and thus gives 'front facade' a ring of redundancy.

facile is usually defined as easy, smooth, without much effort. But the word should contain at least a suggestion of derision. Facile writing isn't just easily read or written, it is also lacking in substance or import. Unless a pejorative sense is intended, the use of *facile* is, to quote Fowler, 'ill-judged'.

factious, factitious. *Factious* applies to factions; it is something that promotes internal bickering or disharmony. *Factitious* applies to that which is artificial or a sham; applause for a despotic ruler may be factitious. Neither should be confused with 'fractious', a term for something that is unruly or disorderly, as in 'a fractious crowd'.

factitious. See FACTIOUS, FACTITIOUS.

fact that. This phrase made Strunk 'quiver with revulsion' and he insisted that it be revised out of every sentence in which it appeared. That may be putting it a trifle strongly. There may be occasions where its use is unavoidable, or at least unexceptionable. But it is true that it does generally signal a sentence that could profitably be recast. 'The court was told that he returned the following night despite the fact that he knew she would not be there' (*Independent*). Try replacing 'despite the fact that' with 'although' or 'even though'. 'Our arrival was delayed for four hours due to the fact that the ferry failed to arrive' (*Sunday Telegraph*). Make it 'because'.

fait accompli. French for an accomplished fact. The plural is *faits accomplis*.

Falange, Phalange. The first is a political party in Spain, the second a political party in Lebanon.

Farrar, Straus & Giroux for the publisher.

farther, further. Insofar as the two are distinguished, *farther* usually appears in contexts involving literal distance ('New York is farther from Sydney than from London') and *further* in contexts involving figurative distance ('I can take this plan no further'). But there is, as the *OED* notes, a large intermediate class of instances in which the choice between the two forms is arbitrary.

faux pas. French for an error or blunder. The plural is also *faux pas*.

faze, meaning to disturb or worry, is sometimes confused with 'phase', as here: 'Christmas doesn't phase me' (*New York Review of Books* headline).

feasible. Not -*able*. The word does not mean probable or plausible, as is sometimes thought, but simply capable of being done. An action can be feasible without being either desirable or likely.

feet, foot. 'First, take a 75-feet hole . . .' (*Daily Mail*); 'Twelve Paraguayan Anaconda snakes, each two foot long . . .' (*The Times*). It should not need pointing out that both of those sentences border on the illiterate.

We do not have 75-feet holes for the same reason that we do not have teethbrushes or horses races. In English, when one noun qualifies another the first is almost always singular. There are exceptions – 'systems analyst', 'singles bar' – but usually they appear only when the normal form would produce ambiguity. When a noun is not being made to function as an adjective (as in the *Times* quotation above), the plural is the usual form. Thus a wall that is six feet high is a six-foot-high wall. For a discussion of the punctuation distinction, see HYPHEN in the Appendix.

fever, temperature. You often hear sentences like 'John had a temperature yesterday' when in fact John has a temperature every day. What he had yesterday was a fever. The distinction is not widely observed, even by some medical authorities. Bernstein cites the instance of a Massachusetts hospital that issued a bulletin stating: 'Everett has no temperature'. Fowler excused the usage as a 'sturdy indefensible', but even so it is better avoided in careful writing, particularly when the remedy has the virtues of simplicity and brevity.

fewer, less. 'In the first four months of the year Rome's tourists were 700,000 less than in the corresponding period last year' (*Guardian*). Probably no other pair of words causes more problems, and with less justification, than *less* and *fewer*. The generally cited rule is that *less* applies to quantity and *fewer* to number. A rougher but more helpful guide is to use *less* with singular nouns (less money, less sugar) and *fewer* with plural nouns (fewer houses, fewer doctors). Thus the quotation above should be either 'Rome's tourists [plural noun] were 700,000 fewer' or 'the number [singular noun] of tourists was 700,000 less'.

A particularly common error is the construction 'no less than', as here: 'There are no less than six bidders for the group' (*The Times*). This construction is so common, in fact, that it could be regarded as having the force of idiom. Philip Howard, for one, allows it when he writes in *Weasel Words*: 'The watch with hands is an analogue device in no less than three different ways'.

Another problem worth noting occurs in this sentence: 'Representatives have offered to produce the supplements on one fewer press than at present' (*The Times*). Idiom, according to Bernstein, doesn't allow 'one fewer press'. You must make it either 'one press fewer', which is more grammatical, or 'one less press', which is more idiomatic.

A final type of problem is seen in this sentence: '. . . but some people earn fewer than $750 a year' (*The Times*). Although $750 is inarguably a plural sum, it functions as a singular. We see it as a totality, not as a collection of individual dollars. Thus the sentence should read 'less than $750'. In the same way it would be wrong to write, 'He lives fewer than fifty miles from London' because fifty miles is being thought of as a total distance and not as fifty individual miles.

filet mignon, but *fillet* for all other dishes and contexts.

filigree for intricate or delicate ornamentation.

finalize is still objected to by many as an ungainly and unnecessary word, and there is no arguing that several other verbs – 'finish', 'complete', 'conclude' – do the job as well without raising hackles.

Finnegans Wake (no apos.) for the 1939 novel by James Joyce.

first and foremost. Choose one.

first, firstly. The question of whether one may write *firstly* or not when beginning a list of points constitutes one of the more inane, but most hotly disputed, issues in the history of English usage. De Quincey called *firstly* 'a ridiculous and most pedantic neologism' and the view has been widely echoed since, though what makes it so objectionable has never been entirely clear, since few object to *secondly*, *thirdly* and so on. Fowler, ever the cool head, should perhaps be allowed the final word on the matter: 'The preference for *first* over *firstly* in formal enumerations is one of the harmless pedantries in which those who like oddities because they are odd are free to indulge, provided that they abstain from censuring those who do not share the liking'.

A separate problem with *first* is seen here: 'The Bangladesh government reacted angrily when plans for blood tests were first announced ... last year' (*Independent*). With words like 'announced', 'reported', 'revealed' and (especially) 'created', *first* is nearly always superfluous, sometimes glaringly so, and should be removed.

firstly. See FIRST, FIRSTLY.

fission. See FUSION, FISSION.

flagrant. See BLATANT, FLAGRANT.

flak. Often misspelled, as here: 'Japanese women take a lot of flack from foreigners for their alleged docility' (*Observer*). The word, for what it is worth, is a contraction of the German *Fliegerabwehr-kanone* ('anti-aircraft gun'), which contains nineteen letters, not one of them a 'c'.

flammable, inflammable. It is an odd inconsistency of English that 'incombustible' describes an object that won't burn, while *inflammable* describes an object that will. Because the meaning of *inflammable* is susceptible to misunderstanding, there is an increasing tendency to use the less ambiguous *flammable*. In other cases this might be considered a regrettable concession to ignorance, but it would be even more regrettable to insist on linguistic purity at the expense of human safety.

flank. 'A Special Report on Finland tomorrow looks at the only Western nation that has to live with the Soviet Union as its neighbour on two flanks' (*The Times*). Two points to note here. The first is that a thing can have only two flanks, so the usage above would be tautological if it weren't inaccurate. The second point is that flanks fall on either side of a body. If I am flanked by people, they are to my left and right. Finland is flanked by the Soviet Union (or at least it was at the time the sentence appeared) and Sweden, and not by the Soviet Union alone, which lay to the east and south.

A similar misusage is seen here: 'The park extends northwards until it is lost to sight, a sea of treetops flanked on each side by enormous, impenetrable cliffs of stone and cement' (*Independent*). Delete 'on each side'. Incidentally, the use of 'cement' in that sentence is also incorrect; see CEMENT, CONCRETE. For a similar error to that involving *flank*, see SURROUNDED.

flaunt, flout. The confusion over these two is so widespread that many dictionaries, particularly in America, have granted them legitimacy as synonyms. To flaunt means to display ostentatiously, to show off. To flout means to treat with contempt, to disregard in a smug manner. There is every reason for keeping these meanings distinct.

floor. See CEILING, FLOOR.

florescent, fluorescent. The first means in flower, the second radiating light.

flotsam and jetsam. In the increasingly unlikely event that you need to distinguish these two, *jetsam* is that part of a shipwreck that has been thrown overboard (think of *jettison*) and *flotsam* that which has floated off of its own accord. (Wreckage found on the sea floor is lagan.) There was a time when the distinction was important: flotsam went to the Crown and jetsam to the lord of the manor on whose land it washed up.

flounder, founder. *Founder* means to sink, either literally (as with a ship) or figuratively (as with a project). *Flounder* means to flail helplessly. It too can be used literally (as with someone struggling in deep water) or figuratively (as with a nervous person making an extemporaneous speech).

flout. See FLAUNT, FLOUT.

fluorescent. See FLORESCENT, FLUORESCENT.

Fogg, Phileas. Not *Phogg*, not *Phineas*, for the character in Jules Verne's 1873 story *Around the World in Eighty Days*.

foot. See FEET, FOOT.

forbear, forebear. The first is a verb meaning to avoid or refrain from. The second is a noun and means ancestor.

forbid, prohibit. The words have the same meaning, but the construction of sentences often dictates which should be used. *Forbid* may be followed only by *to* ('I forbid you to go'). *Prohibit* may not be followed by *to*, but only by *from* ('He was prohibited from going') or by an object noun ('The law prohibits the construction of houses without planning consent'). Thus the following is wrong: 'They are forbidden from uttering any public comments' (*The New York Times*). Make it either 'They are prohibited from uttering . . .' or 'They are forbidden to utter . . .'

forced. See FORCEFUL, FORCIBLE, FORCED.

forceful, forcible, forced. *Forcible* indicates the use of brute force ('forcible entry'). *Forceful* suggests a potential for force ('forceful argument', 'forceful personality'). *Forced* can be used for forcible (as in 'forced entry'), but more often is reserved for actions that are involuntary ('forced march'), or occurring under strain ('forced laughter', 'forced landing').

forcible. See FORCEFUL, FORCIBLE, FORCED.

forebear. See FORBEAR, FOREBEAR.

forego, forgo. Commonly confused, as here: 'Germans are unwilling to forego what many regard as their right to two or three foreign holidays a year' (*Financial Times*). *Forego* means to go before, to precede. To do without is to *forgo*.

forever, for ever. In American usage *forever* is always one word. In Britain traditionally it has been two words (Fowler insisted on it), but more and more dictionaries give *forever* as an alternative or even first choice. The *OED* makes a useful distinction between *for ever* (meaning for all time) and *forever* (meaning continually).

for ever. See FOREVER, FOR EVER.

forgather. 'Wherever people foregather, one hears two kinds of talk . . .' (Simon, *Paradigms Lost*). Although *foregather* is not incorrect, the more usual spelling is *forgather*. A separate question is whether *forgather* adds anything that *gather* alone wouldn't say, apart from a creak of antiquity.

forgo. See FOREGO, FORGO.

former, latter. Properly used, *former* should refer only to the first of two things and *latter* to the second of two things. Thus this extract is incorrect: 'There will be delegates from each of the EEC countries, plus Japan, Singapore, South Korea and Taiwan. Representatives from the latter . . .' (*The Times*). Both words, since they require the reader to hark back to an earlier reference, should be used sparingly and only when what they refer to is immediately evident. Few editing shortcomings are more annoying and less excusable than requiring a reader to re-cover old ground.

fortissimo, fortississimo. The first (abbreviated ff.) means very loud; the second (abbreviated fff.) means as loud as possible.

fortississimo. See FORTISSIMO, FORTISSISSIMO.

fortuitous. Not to be confused with 'fortunate', as it was here: 'If Mr Perella's merger assignment was mostly chance, it nevertheless was fortuitous' (*The New York Times*). *Fortuitous* means accidental or by chance, so the sentence above is telling us that Mr Perella's assignment was not only mostly chance, it was also entirely chance. A fortuitous occurrence may or may not be a fortunate one.

founder. See FLOUNDER, FOUNDER.

fraction. 'The gold recovered so far may represent only a fraction of the total hoard' (*Sunday Times*). A few careful users continue to maintain that *fraction* in the sense of a small part is ambiguous: $\frac{99}{100}$ is also a fraction but hardly a negligible part. The looser usage, however, has been around for at least 300 years (Shakespeare uses it in *Troilus and Cressida*) and is unlikely to be misunderstood in most contexts. Even so, it would be more precise to say 'a small part' or 'a tiny part'. (See also PERCENTAGE, PROPORTION.)

Frankfurt am Main is the formal name of the German city that serves as the nation's financial centre. It should be remembered that there is a second Frankfurt in Germany, Frankfurt an der Oder, and that the two may sometimes need to be distinguished. (Note particularly that one uses *am*, the other *an*). It is perhaps also worth noting that most American communities, including the capital of Kentucky, spell the name Frankfort.

Frazer-Nash for the British sports car. Not *Fraser-*.

fresh. Usually the word serves as an unobjectionable synonym for 'new', but it has additional connotations that make it inappropriate in some contexts, as the following vividly demonstrates: 'Three weeks after the earthquake, fresh bodies have been found in the wreckage' (cited by Spiegl in *The Joy of Words*).

Friesian, Frisian. *Friesian* is a breed of cattle; *Frisian* is a north Germanic language and the name of a chain of islands lying off, and politically divided between, The Netherlands, Denmark and Germany. Friesian cattle in the US are normally called Holsteins. *Frisian* is also sometimes applied to people from Friesland, the Dutch province that partly encompasses the Frisian islands.

Frisian. See FRIESIAN, FRISIAN.

frisson. 'A slight frisson went through the nation yesterday' (*The Times*). There is no other kind of frisson than a slight one. The word means shiver or shudder.

frontbench. See FRONT BENCH, FRONTBENCH.

front bench (noun), **frontbench** (adj.). In politics, a senior member sits on the front bench, but is a frontbench spokesman. The same pattern holds true, of course, for back bench.

frowsty, frowzy. The first means musty or stale, the second untidy or dingy.

frowzy. See FROWSTY, FROWZY.

Fujiyama means 'Mount Fuji', so Mount Fujiyama is redundant. Use either Fujiyama or Mount Fuji. The Japanese also call it Fujisan and Fuki-no-Yama.

fulsome is one of the most frequently misapplied words in English. The sense that is usually accorded it – of being abundant or unstinting – is almost the opposite of the word's dictionary meaning. *Fulsome* is related to foul and means odious or overfull, offensively insincere. 'Fulsome praise', properly used, isn't a lavish tribute; it is unctuous and insincere toadying.

further. See FARTHER, FURTHER.

fusion, fission. Both describe ways of producing nuclear energy: *fusion* by fusing two light nuclei into a single, heavier nucleus; *fission* by splitting the nucleus of an atom.

future. As an adjective, the word is often used unnecessarily: 'He refused to say what his future plans were' (*Daily Telegraph*); 'The parties are prepared to say little about how they see their future prospects' (*The Times*). In both sentences, and nearly all others like them, *future* adds nothing and should be deleted.

G

gabardine, gaberdine. The first is a type of cloth, the second a long cloak.

gaberdine. See GABARDINE, GABERDINE.

gambit is often misused in either of two ways. First, it sometimes appears as 'opening gambit', which is redundant. Second, it is often employed to mean no more than a ploy or tactic. Properly, a gambit is an opening move that involves some strategic sacrifice or concession. All gambits are opening moves, but not all opening moves are gambits.

gamy. Not -*ey*.

Gasthaus, Gasthof. The first is German for an inn or guest house; the second is German for a hotel. The plurals are *Gasthäuser* and *Gasthöfe*.

Gasthof. See GASTHAUS, GASTHOF.

gateau (or gâteau). The plural is *gateaus* (or *gâteaux*).

geezer, geyser. The first is British slang for an old man; the second is a source of hot water, as in a thermal spring or, in Britain, a household boiler. *Geyser* rhymes with *sneezer* in Britain and with *miser* in the US.

gendarmes. Some popular dictionaries define *gendarmes* as French police officers. In fact, gendarmes are soldiers employed in police duties, principally in the countryside. Police officers in French cities and towns are just that – police officers.

gender. 'A university grievance committee decided that she had been denied tenure because of her gender' (*The New York Times*). *Gender*, originally strictly a grammatical term, became in the nineteenth century a euphemism for the convenience of those who found 'sex' too disturbing a word to utter. Its use today in that sense is disdained by most authorities as old-fashioned and over-delicate.

genus, species. The second is a subgroup of the first. The convention is to capitalize the genus but not the species, as in *Homo sapiens*. The plurals are *genera* and *species*.

Georgetown. See GEORGE TOWN, GEORGETOWN.

George Town, Georgetown. The first is capital of the Cayman Islands and the principal city of the island and state of Penang in Malaysia. The second is capital of Guyana and a district and university in Washington, DC.

germane, relevant, material. *Germane* and *relevant* are synonymous. Both indicate a pertinence to the matter under discussion. *Material* has the additional connotation of being necessary. A material point is one without which an argument would be incomplete. A germane or relevant point will be worth noting but may not be essential to the argument.

gerrymander is to distort or redraw to one's advantage, especially political boundaries. Not to be confused with *jerry-built*.

gerunds are verbs made to function as nouns, as with the italicized words in 'I don't like *dancing*' and '*Cooking* is an art'. Two problems commonly arise with gerunds:

    1. Sometimes the gerund is unnecessarily set off by an article

and preposition, as here: 'They said that *the* valuing *of* the paintings could take several weeks' (*Daily Telegraph*). Deleting the italicized words would make the sentence shorter and more forceful.

2. Problems also occur when a possessive noun or pronoun (called a 'genitive') qualifies a gerund. A common type of construction is seen here: 'They objected to him coming'. Properly it should be: 'They objected to his coming'. Similarly, 'There is little hope of Smith gaining admittance to the club' should be 'There is little hope of Smith's gaining admittance . . .'.

The possessive form is, in short, the preferred form, especially with proper nouns and personal pronouns. For Fowler (who treated the matter under the heading 'fused participle') the possessive was virtually the only form. He insisted, for instance, on 'We cannot deny the possibility of anything's happening' and 'This will result in many's having to go into lodgings'. Most other authorities regard this as a Fowler idiosyncrasy, and the position was quietly and sensibly abandoned in the third (and most recent) edition.

geyser. See GEEZER, GEYSER.

Ghanaian for a person from Ghana.

ghettos. Not *-oes*.

gild the lily. The passage from Shakespeare's *King John* is: 'To gild refined gold, to paint the lily . . . / Is wasteful and ridiculous excess'. Thus it is both wrong and resorting to a woeful cliché to speak of 'gilding the lily' in the sense of overdoing something.

goodbye. One word.

goodwill. See GOOD WILL, GOODWILL.

good will, goodwill. Either form is acceptable in general senses, but it is always one word when referring to the reputation and trading value of a business.

gourmand is a word to be used carefully. Some dictionaries now define it only as a person who likes to eat well, but others equate it with gluttony. Unless you mean to convey a pejorative sense, it would be better to use 'gourmet', 'gastronome', 'epicure' or some other more flattering term.

graffiti. 'There was graffiti in glorious abundance' (*Daily Mail*). It is probably a losing battle, but I think it still worth pointing out that *graffiti* is a plural and that the sentence would be better as 'There were graffiti . . .'. If all you mean is a single embellishment, the term is *graffito*.

grammatical error as a term is sometimes objected to on the grounds that a word or phrase cannot be simultaneously grammatical and erroneous, but must be either one or the other. In fact, the primary meaning of *grammatical* is 'of or relating to grammar', which includes errors of grammar, and in any case the expression is well established.

grandiloquence, not *-eloquence*, for inflated speech.

greater. Sometimes a pointer to wordiness, as here: 'The cost for a 17-year-old living in the greater London area . . .' (*The Times*). 'In greater London' or 'the London area' says the same thing as 'in the greater London area', but says it more simply.

grief, grieve. 'As U.S. Travel Abroad Drops, Europe Grieves' (*New York Times* headline). Did it? Europe may have been alarmed at, suffered from, fretted or worried over the loss of American tourist revenue, but is it reasonable to suggest that there was grief attached? Similar strong, emotive words – 'mourn', 'ravage', 'anguish' and so on – are better reserved for strong, emotive contexts. (See also PLEA, PLEAD.)

grieve. See GRIEF, GRIEVE.

grievous. The word is not *grievious*, though it is often so misspelled, as here: 'He admitted robbery and causing grievious bodily harm and was jailed for seven years' (*Independent*). A similar error occurs with 'mischievous', which is sometimes misspelled – and even mispronounced – as 'mischievious'.

grisly, gristly, grizzly. Occasionally and variously confused. The first means horrifying or gruesome. The second applies to meat that is full of gristle. The third means grey, especially grey-haired, and is a cliché when applied to old men.

gristly. See GRISLY, GRISTLY, GRIZZLY.

grizzly. See GRISLY, GRISTLY, GRIZZLY.

gross domestic product, gross national product. Gross domestic product is everything produced by a nation during a given period except earnings from overseas. Gross national product is everything produced by a nation during a given period including earnings from overseas.

gross national product. See GROSS DOMESTIC PRODUCT, GROSS NATIONAL PRODUCT.

growth. Often used contrarily by economists and those who write about them: 'It now looks as if growth will remain stagnant until spring' (*Observer*); '. . . with the economy moving into a negative growth phase' (*The Times*). *Growth* obviously indicates expansion. If a thing is shrinking or standing still, *growth* simply isn't the word for it.

Guadalupe, Guadeloupe. The cluster of islands in the Caribbean, which together form an overseas department of France, is Guadeloupe. Most other geographical features bearing the name, including a river and range of mountains in the south-western United States, and towns or cities in Spain, Peru, the Azores and California, spell it Guadalupe.

Guadeloupe. See GUADALUPE, GUADELOUPE.

Guangdong, Guangzhou. Guangdong is the Chinese province formerly known as Kwantung. Its capital is Guangzhou, formerly Canton.

Guangzhou. See GUANGDONG, GUANGZHOU.

Guiana, Guyana. Some scope for confusion here, particularly if using old references. The name Guiana has at various times been attached to three contiguous territories on the Atlantic coast of northern South America. The westernmost, British Guiana, is now called Guyana. The central territory, Dutch Guiana, is now Suriname. The easternmost, an overseas department of France, remains French Guiana.

Guinea, Guinea-Bissau, Equatorial Guinea. They are separate countries, all in west Africa. Guinea was formerly French Guinea. Guinea-Bissau was formerly Portuguese Guinea. Equatorial Guinea was formerly Spanish Guinea.

Guinea-Bissau. See GUINEA, GUINEA-BISSAU, EQUATORIAL GUINEA.

guttural. Not *-er*.

Guyana. See GUIANA, GUYANA.

H

Häagen-Dazs for the ice cream.

Haarlem, Netherlands, but *Harlem*, New York.

habits. 'As was his usual habit . . .' (*Sunday Express*); 'The customary habits of the people of the South Pacific . . .' (*Daily Telegraph*). Habits are always customary and always usual. That is, of course, what makes them habitual.

had better. 'When the London summit meets, foreign ministers better stiffen their sinews' (*Guardian*). In conditional sentences like that one, the required expression is *had better*. The error, more common in America than in Britain, is seen again in this advertisement in *The New York Times*: 'It will go 799 miles between gas stations. It better be the world's most comfortable car'. Make it 'it had better be' or at least 'it'd better be'.

haemorrhage. Note -*rr*-. The American spelling is *hemorrhage*.

haemorrhoids. Note -*rr*-. The American spelling is *hemorrhoids*.

hail, hale. *Hale* means robust and vigorous, or to drag or forcibly draw (as in 'haled into court'), in which sense it is related to *haul*. *Hail* describes a greeting, a salute or a downpour. The expressions are 'hale and hearty' and 'hail-fellow-well-met'.

haka for the Maori war dance widely associated with New Zealand sporting appearances.

hale. See HAIL, HALE.

hamlet. 'Police searched his house in the tiny hamlet of Oechtringen . . .' (*Observer*). It is in the nature of hamlets to be tiny.

handiwork. Not *handy-*.

hangar, not *-er*, for the place where aircraft are stored.

hanged. 'It was disclosed that a young white official had been found hanged to death in his cell . . .' (*The New York Times*). 'Hanged to death' is redundant. So too, for that matter, are 'starved to death' and 'strangled to death'. The writer was correct, however, in saying that the official had been found *hanged* and not *hung*. People are hanged; pictures and the like are hung.

Hansard. Formally, it is *The Official Report of Parliamentary Debates.*

hara-kiri is the correct spelling for the ritual form of suicide involving disembowelment. In Japan, it is normally known as *seppuku.*

harangue, tirade. Each is sometimes used when the other is intended. A tirade is always abusive and can be directed at one person or at several. A harangue, however, need not be vituperative, but may merely be prolonged and tedious. It does, however, require at least two listeners. One person cannot, properly speaking, harangue another.

harass. Note one 'r' and *-ss*.

harebrained, harelipped. Not *hair-*.

harelipped. See HAREBRAINED, HARELIPPED.

hark, but *hearken*.

hartebeest for the African antelope. Not *-beast*.

Harz Mountains, Germany. Not *Hartz*.

Hasselblad for the Swedish cameras.

Hawker Siddeley (no hyphen) for the British aviation company.

head over heels is not just a cliché; it is also, when you think about it, a faintly absurd one. Our heads are usually over our heels.

healthful. See HEALTHY, HEALTHFUL, SALUTARY.

healthy, healthful, salutary. Some authorities maintain that *healthy* should apply only to those things that possess health and *healthful* to those that promote it. Thus we would have 'healthy children', but 'healthful food' and 'healthful exercise'. There is no harm in observing the distinction, but there is little to be gained from insisting on it. If we are to become resolute, it would be better to focus on *healthy* in the sense of big or vigorous, as in 'a healthy wage increase', which is both inexact and overworked.

Salutary has a wider meaning than either of the other words. It too means conducive to health, but can also apply to anything that is demonstrably beneficial ('a salutary lesson in etiquette'). Most often, however, it is used to describe actions or properties that have a remedial influence: 'The new drug has a salutary effect on arthritis'.

hear, hear! is the exclamation of parliamentarians, not *here, here!*

Hebrew, Yiddish. The two languages have almost nothing in common except that they are spoken primarily by Jewish people. Yiddish (from the German *jüdisch*, 'Jewish') is a modified German dialect and thus a part of the Indo-European family of languages.

Hebrew is a Semitic tongue and therefore is more closely related to Arabic. Yiddish writers sometimes use the Hebrew alphabet, but the two languages are no more closely related than, say, English and Swahili.

Heidsieck for the champagne.

heir apparent, heir presumptive. The first inherits no matter what; the second inherits only if a nearer relation is not born first.

heir presumptive. See HEIR APPARENT, HEIR PRESUMPTIVE.

Helens, St. Both St Helens, Merseyside, and Mount St Helens, the volcanic mountain in Washington state, US, are without an apostrophe.

hiccough. See HICCUP, HICCOUGH.

hiccup, hiccough. The first is now generally the preferred spelling.

highfalutin (no apos.) is the correct – or at least the standard – spelling, though many dictionaries also accept *highfaluting*, *highfaluten* and *hifalutin*. The word has been around for about 130 years, but is still considered informal by most sources. Its origin is uncertain.

high jinks, two words, is the usual spelling, though some dictionaries also accept *hijinks*. The derivation is unknown but it is not related to (or to be confused with) 'jinx' as in bad luck. The word can be used as either a singular or plural.

high street. Unless you are talking about a specific high street, there is no reason to give it initial caps.

Hindi, Hindu, Hinduism, Hindustani. Hindi is the main language of India and Hindustani is its main dialect. Hinduism is the main religious and social system of India. Hindu describes a follower of Hinduism.

hindrance. Not *-erance*.

Hindu. See HINDI, HINDU, HINDUISM, HINDUSTANI.

Hinduism. See HINDI, HINDU, HINDUISM, HINDUSTANI.

Hindustani. See HINDI, HINDU, HINDUISM, HINDUSTANI.

hippie. Not *-ppy*.

hippopotamuses is the plural of hippopotamus.

Hirshhorn Museum, Washington, DC. Note *-hh-*.

historic, historical. 'The Landmarks Preservation Commission voted yesterday to create a historical district on a gilded stretch of Manhattan's East Side' (*The New York Times*). Something that makes history or is part of history, as in the example above, is historic. Something that is based on history or describes history is historical ('a historical novel'). A historic judicial ruling is one that makes history; a historical ruling is based on precedent. There are, however, at least two exceptions to the rule – in accountancy ('historic costs') and, curiously, in grammar ('historic tenses'). (See also A, AN.)

historical. See HISTORIC, HISTORICAL.

hitchhike, hitchhiker. Note *-hh-*.

hitchhiker. See HITCHHIKE, HITCHHIKER.

hitherto. 'In 1962, the regime took the hitherto unthinkable step of appropriating land' (*Daily Telegraph*). The writer meant 'thitherto' ('until then'), but 'theretofore' would have been better and 'previously' better still.

hoard, horde. Often confused, as here: 'Chrysler Corp. has a cash horde of \$1.5 billion' (*Time* magazine). An accumulation of valuables, often hidden, is a *hoard*. *Horde* originally described nomadic tribes, but now applies to any crowd, particularly to a thronging and disorganized one ('hordes of Christmas shoppers').

hoary, not -*ey*, for something that is grey or aged.

Hobson's choice is sometimes taken to mean a dilemma or difficult decision, but in fact means no choice at all. It derives from a sixteenth-century Cambridge stable-keeper named Thomas Hobson, who hired out horses on a strict rotation. The customer was allowed to take the one nearest the stable door or none at all.

Hoffmann, The Tales of. See TALES OF HOFFMANN, THE.

hoi polloi. Two problems here. The first is that *hoi polloi* means the masses, the common populace, and not the elite as is often thought. The second problem is that in Greek *hoi* means 'the', so to speak of 'the hoi polloi' is tantamount to saying 'the the masses'. The best answer to both problems is to substitute another, less troublesome term.

holocaust. In Greek the word means 'burnt whole' and, generally speaking, it is better reserved for disasters involving fiery destruction. You should not, for instance, use the word to describe the devastation wrought by a hurricane or mudslide. However, a clear exception is in references to the slaughter of Jews by Germany during the Second World War, when it describes the entire extermination process. In such contexts, the word is normally capitalized.

homely. Occasionally a source of confusion between Britons and

Americans. In Britain the word means comfortable and appealing, but in America it means unattractive and unappealing, so take care which sense is intended.

homogeneous, homogenous. 'It is . . . the only practical wind instrument, giving 5½ octaves of homogenous sound' (*Guardian*). *Homogenous* normally should be confined to biological contexts, where it describes organisms having common ancestry. *Homogeneous* describes things that are consistent and uniform, the sense clearly intended in the example.

homogenous. See HOMOGENEOUS, HOMOGENOUS.

homonym, homophone. Both describe words that have strong similarities of sound or spelling, but different meanings. A *homophone* is a word that sounds like another but has a different meaning or spelling or both. A *homonym* is a word that also has a different meaning, but the same spelling or sound. Thus 'blue' and 'blew' are both homonyms and homophones. However, 'bow' as in a ship and 'bow' as in a tie are homonyms (because they are spelled the same) but not homophones (because they have different pronunciations). In short, unless the intention is to emphasize the equivalence of pronunciations, *homonym* is generally the better word.

homophone. See HOMONYM, HOMOPHONE.

honorariums, not *honoraria*, is generally the preferred plural for honorarium.

hopefully. 'To travel hopefully is a better thing than to arrive'. Fifty years ago that sentence by Robert Louis Stevenson would have suggested only one interpretation: that it is better to travel filled with hope than to actually reach your destination. Today, however, it could also be read as meaning: 'To travel is, I hope, better than arriving'.

This extended sense of *hopefully* has been condemned with some passion by many authorities, among them Philip Howard, who calls it, 'ambiguous and obscure, as well as illiterate and ugly'. Many others, notably Bernstein and Gowers, accept it, though usually only grudgingly and often with restrictions attached.

Most of those who object to *hopefully* in its looser sense do so on the argument that it is a misused modal auxiliary – that is to say, that it fails to modify the elements it should. Take the sentence 'Hopefully the sun will come out soon'. As constructed that sentence suggests (at least to a literal-minded person) that it is the sun whose manner is hopeful, not yours or mine. After all, you would hardly say, 'Believably the sun will come out soon' if you believed it might or 'Thinkingly the sun will come out soon' if you thought as much or 'Hopelessly . . .' if you hoped it wouldn't.

The shortcoming of that argument is that those writers who scrupulously avoid *hopefully* do not hesitate to use at least a dozen other words – 'apparently', 'presumably', 'happily', 'sadly', 'mercifully', 'thankfully' and many others – in precisely the same way. In *Paradigms Lost*, the American critic John Simon roundly disdains the looser *hopefully*, yet elsewhere he writes: 'Marshall Sahlins, who professes anthropology at the University of Chicago, errs some 15 times in an admittedly long piece'. That 'admittedly' is as unattached as any *hopefully* ever was.

To accept the one while excusing the other is, I submit, curious and illogical and more than a little reminiscent of those Victorian purists who insisted that 'laughable' should be 'laugh-at-able' and that grammatical virtue would be served by turning 'reliable' into 'relionable'.

There are, however, two other grounds for regarding *hopefully* with suspicion. The first is that, as in the Stevenson quotation at the beginning of this entry, it introduces a possibility of ambiguity. Gowers cites this sentence: 'Our team will start their innings hopefully immediately after tea'. It isn't possible to say whether *hopefully* refers to the team's frame of mind or to the time it will start batting.

A second objection is to the lameness of the word. If a newspaper report says, 'Hopefully the dockers' strike will end today', who exactly is doing the hoping? The writer? The dockers? All right-minded people? All too often the word is used as no more than an easy escape from having to take responsibility for a sentiment and as such is to be deplored.

But the real issue with *hopefully* has more to do with fashion than with linguistic rectitude. *The American Heritage Dictionary*, after noting that there are no real grounds to object to the extended sense of *hopefully*, adds with an all but audible sigh: 'However, this usage is by now such a bugbear to traditionalists that it is best avoided on grounds of civility, if not logic'.

horde. See HOARD, HORDE.

hors-d'oeuvre for an appetizer. The plural is *hors-d'oeuvres*.

hovercraft (no cap.). The name is no longer a trade mark.

Howards End (no apos.) for the 1910 novel by E. M. Forster.

Hudson Bay, Hudson River, Hudson Strait, but *Hudson's Bay Company.*

Hudson River. See HUDSON BAY, HUDSON RIVER, HUDSON STRAIT.

Hudson Strait. See HUDSON BAY, HUDSON RIVER, HUDSON STRAIT.

humerus is the spelling for the bone between the elbow and shoulder. The plural is *humeri*.

I

I, me. 'It was a bizarre little scenario – the photographer and me ranged on one side, the petulant actor and his agent on the other' (*Sunday Times*). At least the next sentence didn't begin: 'Me turned to the actor and asked him . . .'. Make it, obviously, 'the photographer and I'.

Probably the most common problem with *I* and *me*, and certainly the most widely disputed, is deciding whether to write 'It was I' or 'It was me'. The more liberal authorities are inclined to allow 'It was me' on the argument that it is more colloquial and less affected, while the prescriptivists lean towards 'It was I' on the indisputable grounds that it is more grammatical. A point generally overlooked by both sides is that 'It is I' and like constructions are often both graceless and wordy. Instead of writing 'It was he who was nominated' or 'It is she whom I love', why not simply say, 'He was nominated' or 'I love her'?

Things become more troublesome still when a subordinate clause is influenced contradictorily by a personal pronoun and a relative pronoun, as here: 'It is not you who is [are?] angry'. 'Is' is grammatically correct, but again the sentence would be less stilted if recast as 'You are not the one who is angry' or 'You aren't angry'. (See also IT.)

idée fixe is French for an obsession or fixation. The plural is *idées fixes*.

idiosyncrasy. One of the most commonly misspelled of all words, especially in the plural, and it is always misspelled in the same way: 'Most of the statistics about Texas reflect the idiosyncracies of the Lone Star state, not George W. Bush's achievements or failures' (*Economist*); 'At the same time, the international fashion world . . . has accepted the idiosyncracies of the British' (*The New York Times*). Note that the penultimate consonant is an 's', not a 'c'.

i.e. See E.G., I.E.

if. Problems often arise in deciding whether *if* is introducing a subjunctive clause ('If I were . . .') or an indicative one ('If I was . . .'). The distinction is straightforward. When *if* introduces a notion that is hypothetical or improbable or clearly untrue, the verb should be in the subjunctive: 'If I were king . . .'; 'If he were in your shoes . . .'. But when the *if* is introducing a thought that is true or could well be true, the mood should be indicative: 'If I was happy then, I certainly am not now'. One small hint: if the sentence contains *would* or *wouldn't*, the mood is subjunctive, as in 'If I were you, I wouldn't take the job'. (See also SUBJUNCTIVES.)

if and when. Almost always unnecessary. Choose one or the other.

ileum, ilium. The ileum is part of the small intestine; the ilium is part of the pelvis. Ilium (cap. I) is also the Latin name for Troy.

ilium. See ILEUM, ILIUM.

immoral. See AMORAL, IMMORAL.

impel. See COMPEL, IMPEL.

imply, infer. 'Speaking on ABC-TV's *Good Morning America*, Mrs Bush inferred that Clinton had brought disrespect to the presidency' (*Los Angeles Times*). According to nearly all authorities, on both sides of the Atlantic, the word there should be *implied*, not *inferred*. *Imply* means to suggest: 'He implied that I was a fool'. *Infer* means to deduce: 'After three hours of waiting, we inferred that they weren't coming'. A speaker implies, a listener infers. The distinction is useful and, in careful writing nowadays, expected. However, it must be pointed out that there is not a great deal of historical basis for the distinction. Many great writers, among them Milton, Sir Thomas More, Jane Austen and Shakespeare, freely used *infer* where we would today insist on *imply*. Indeed, until as late as 1976, *The Concise Oxford Dictionary* treated the words as interchangeable. None the less, to use *infer* where most educated people now expect *imply* is to invite derision.

important, importantly. 'But more importantly, his work was instrumental in eradicating cholera' (*Sunday Telegraph*). Some authorities condemn *importantly* with the argument that the sentence contains an ellipsis of thought – that in effect it is saying, 'But [what is] more important . . .'. Others contend that *importantly* functions as a sentence adverb, modifying the whole expression, in much the same way as 'happily' in 'Happily, it didn't rain'. Both points are grammatically defensible, so the choice of which to use must be entirely a matter of preference.

importantly. See IMPORTANT, IMPORTANTLY.

imports, exports. Here is a common lapse in an unexpected place: 'America's booming economy has sucked in imports from abroad' (*Economist*). It is implicit in imports that their source is foreign. Delete 'from abroad'. Similar phrases involving exports, such as 'British exports to overseas countries' (*Guardian*), equally call out for pruning.

impracticable. See IMPRACTICAL, IMPRACTICABLE, UN-PRACTICAL.

impractical, impracticable, unpractical. If a thing could be done but isn't worth doing, it is impractical or unpractical (the words mean the same). If it can't be done at all, it's impracticable (the word means 'incapable of being put into practice').

impromptu. See EXTEMPORE, IMPROMPTU.

in, into, in to. Generally, *in* indicates a fixed position ('he was in the house') while *into* indicates movement towards a fixed position ('he went into the house'). There are, however, many exceptions (e.g., 'he put it in his pocket'). As so often with idiom, there is no describable pattern to these exceptions; it is just the way it is.

Whether to write *into* as one word or two also sometimes causes problems. The simple rule is that *in to* (two words) is correct when *in* is an adverb, but the distinction can perhaps best be seen in paired examples: 'He turned himself into [one word] an accomplished artist' but 'The criminal turned himself in to [two words] the police'.

inadmissible. Not *-able*.

inasmuch, but *in so far*, in British usage. In American usage, *insofar* is one word.

inchoate. Probably because of the similarity in spelling to *chaotic* and in pronunciation to *incoherent*, people sometimes take the word to mean disorderly or disorganized. In fact, it means incipient, undeveloped, just starting. An inchoate enterprise is likely to be disorganized, but the disorderliness is not what makes it inchoate.

incline. As a verb, *incline* indicates a conscious decision, as in 'They were inclined to go to Greece for the summer'. When no choice is involved, *incline* is incorrect, as it was here: 'Roads are inclined to deteriorate during bad weather' (*Daily Telegraph*).

include indicates that what is to follow is only part of a greater whole. To use it when you are describing a totality is sloppy: 'The company's three main operating divisions, which include hotels, catering and package holidays . . .' (*Guardian*); 'The 630 job losses include 300 in Redcar and 330 in Port Talbot' (*The Times*).

incomprehensible. Not *-able*.

inculcate means to persistently impress a habit upon or belief into another person. You inculcate an idea, not a person. 'My father inculcated me with a belief in democracy' should be 'My father inculcated in me a belief in democracy'.

indefinitely. 'The new structures should, by contrast, last almost indefinitely' (*Newsweek*). *Indefinitely* in the sense of 'for a very long time' is almost always better avoided. The word means only 'without prescribed limits'. Thus, strictly speaking, the sentence above is telling us that the structures may last for a million years or they may collapse next week. 'Almost indefinitely', incidentally, is impossible.

indexes, indices. Either is acceptable, though some dictionaries favour *indices* for technical applications.

indices. See INDEXES, INDICES.

indict, indite. Very occasionally confused, as here: '. . . the American Family Association persuaded the city council to indite the museum director and his board for obscenity' (*Independent*). To lay a formal charge, the sense intended here, is to *indict*. *Indite*, a word rare almost to the point of obsolescence, means to set down in writing.

indispensable. Not *-ible*.

indite. See INDICT, INDITE.

individual is unexceptionable when you are contrasting one person with an organization or body of people ('How can one individual hope to rectify the evils of society?'). But as a simple synonym for person ('Do you see that individual standing over there?') it is still generally frowned on by British authorities as casual and inelegant.

indubitably. See DOUBTLESS, UNDOUBTEDLY, INDUBITABLY.

infectious. See CONTAGIOUS, INFECTIOUS.

infer. See IMPLY, INFER.

inflammable. See FLAMMABLE, INFLAMMABLE.

inflation has become so pleasantly quiescent in recent years that the word and its several variant forms are much less often used than they were when this book first appeared. However (and just in case), it is worth noting a few definitions. *Inflation* itself means that the money supply and prices are rising. *Hyper-inflation* means that they are rising rapidly (at an annual rate of at least 20 per cent). *Deflation* means that they are falling, and *reflation* that they are being pushed up again after a period of deflation. *Stagflation* means that prices are rising while output is stagnant. *Disinflation*, a word so vague in sense to most readers that it is almost always better avoided, means that prices are rising but at a rate slower than before. Finally, bear in mind that if the rate of inflation was 4.5 per cent last month and 3.5 per cent this month, it does not mean that prices are falling; they are rising at a slower rate.

innocent. 'She and four other inmates have pleaded innocent to the tax charges' (*Boston Globe*). Under the British and American judicial systems, people do not plead innocent. They plead guilty or not guilty.

in order to. A wordy locution even in the hands of an authority: 'Grammar may be defined as the system of principles . . . according to which words must be patterned in order to be understood' (Shipley, *In Praise of English*). Removing *in order* would shorten the sentence without altering the sense. (See also IN, INTO, IN TO.)

inquiry. See QUERY, INQUIRY, ENQUIRY.

insidious, invidious. *Insidious* indicates the stealthy spread of something undesirable ('an insidious leak in the pipe'). *Invidious* means offensive or inviting animosity ('I was angered by his invidious remarks').

in spite of. See DESPITE, IN SPITE OF.

intense, intensive. *Intense* should describe things that are heavy or extreme or occur to a high degree (intense sunlight, intense downpour). *Intensive* implies a concentrated focus (intensive care, an intensive search). Although the two words often come to the same thing, they needn't. An intense bombardment, as Fowler has pointed out, is a severe one. An intensive bombardment is one directed at a small (or relatively small) area.

intensive. See INTENSE, INTENSIVE.

International Atomic Energy Agency. Not *Authority.*

international courts. Understandably, these sometimes cause confusion. The International Court of Justice, or World Court, in The Hague is an offspring of the United Nations and deals with disputes between or among UN member states. The European Court of Justice, in Luxembourg, is a European Union institution dealing exclusively with disputes involving EU member states. The European Court of Human Rights, in Strasbourg, addresses issues of civil liberties arising from the European Convention on Human Rights. It has no connection with the United Nations or European Union.

International Olympic Committee. Not *Olympics.*

internecine. For more than 200 years writers have used *internecine* in the sense of a costly or self-destructive conflict even though etymologically the word signifies only a slaughter or massacre without any explicit sense of cost to the victor. For this small error, we can thank Samuel Johnson, who was misled by the prefix *inter-* and defined the word as 'endeavouring mutual destruction'. However, it has been misused for so long that it would be pedantic and wildly optimistic to try to enforce its original meaning. As Philip Howard has noted: 'The English language cannot be regulated so as to avoid offending the susceptibilities of classical scholars'. He does suggest, however, that the word should be reserved for bloody and violent disputes and not mere squabblings.

interval. '. . . the training period was still three years, an interval widely regarded in the industry as being unrealistically long' (cited by Gowers). An interval is the period *between* two events.

into. See IN, INTO, IN TO.

in to. See IN, INTO, IN TO.

intrigue. Originally *intrigue* signified underhanded plotting and nothing else. The looser meaning of arousing or fascinating ('We found the lecture intriguing') is now established. It is, however, greatly overworked and almost always better replaced by a more telling word.

invariably does not mean frequently or usually, as was intended here: 'Supersede is yet another word that is invariably misspelled' (*Chicago Tribune*). It means fixed, constant, not subject to change – in short, without variance. Night invariably follows day, but no word is invariably misspelled.

inveigh, inveigle. Occasionally confused. The first means to speak strongly against ('He inveighed against the rise in taxes'). The second means to entice or cajole ('They inveigled an invitation to the party').

inveigle. See INVEIGH, INVEIGLE.

invidious. See INSIDIOUS, INVIDIOUS.

irony, sarcasm. *Irony* is the use of words to convey a contradiction between the literal and intended meanings. *Sarcasm* is very like irony except that it is more stinging. Where the primary intent behind irony is to amuse, with sarcasm it is to wound or score points.

irregardless. There is no such word. Make it *regardless*.

ise/-ize. In British usage whether verbs end in *-ise* or *-ize* (e.g. recognise or recognize) is normally a matter of preference or house style. Many publishers use *-ize* endings, as does this dictionary. However, even under the *-ize* system several verbs always end in *-ise*, of which the following are the main ones: advertise, apprise, chastise, circumcise, comprise, compromise, demise, despise, devise, disguise, excise, exercise, franchise, improvise, incise, merchandise, premise, reprise, supervise, surmise, surprise, televise.

A separate issue concerns objections often raised by authorities to words like finalize, hospitalize and prioritize. Although the English language has been forming such words for centuries – bastardize, for instance, dates from the 1500s – new formations almost always encounter sustained opposition. Strunk in 1935 attacked prioritize and customize. Gowers in 1965 expressed dislike for finalize, among many others. Several usage books continue to disdain hospitalize. The arguments brought against many of these formations can have a somewhat ironic ring because what is elsewhere welcomed as a virtue – brevity – is suddenly considered not so important. Certainly there can be no denying that prioritize is shorter than 'make a priority of' and hospitalize less cumbersome than 'admit to a hospital'. The only honest objection to such words is that they are jarring or faddish. The protests are more convincing where a short verb form already exists. There is no special excuse for *moisturize* when we already have *moisten*, or for *finalize* when we have *finish*. The general principle, as with most matters of usage, should be that the word should not draw undue attention to itself by its novelty or air of contrivance.

it. Sentences that begin with *it* are almost always worth a second look. Oftentimes an anticipatory or 'dummy' *it* is unobjectionable ('It seems to me', 'It began to rain', 'It is widely believed that'), but just as often it is no more than a sign of careless or tedious writing, as here: 'It was Mr Bechtel who was the more peripatetic of the two'; 'It was under his direction that the annual reports began' (*The New York Times*). Both sentences would be shorter and more forceful if 'It was' and the relative pronouns (respectively 'who' and 'that') were removed, making them 'Mr Bechtel was the more peripatetic of the two' and 'Under his direction the annual reports began'.

its, it's. The distinction between these two ought not to trouble a ten-year-old, yet errors abound, particularly outside formal writing. *Its* is the possessive form of *it*: 'Put each book in its place'. *It's* is the contraction of *it is*: 'The beauty of solar power is that it's environmentally friendly'.

it's. See ITS, IT'S.

-ize. See -ISE/-IZE.

J

James's, St, for the palace, park and square in London. Not *James'*.

jargon, argot, lingua franca. At a conference of American sociologists in 1977, 'love' was defined as 'the cognitive-affective state characterized by intrusive fantasizing concerning reciprocity of amorant feelings by the object of the amorance'. That is *jargon* – the practice of never calling a spade a spade when you might instead call it a manual earth-restructuring implement. So long as it circulates only among a given profession, jargon is usually unobjectionable and frequently useful, since every profession needs its own form of shorthand. But all too often it escapes into the wider world, so that we encounter 'attitudinal constructs' when what is meant is attitudes and 'optimally consonant patterns of learning' for a sound education. In this sense, jargon is always better avoided.

Argot was originally the language of thieves, but has, like jargon, come to mean a way of communicating peculiar to a particular group. *Lingua franca* (literally 'the Frankish tongue') is any language or mixture of languages that serves as a common means of communication among diverse parties. English, for instance, is the lingua franca of international air travel.

jeep, Jeep. Use *jeep* generally for army vehicles, but *Jeep* specifically for the brand name of cars produced by the German-American company DaimlerChrysler.

jerry-built, jury-rigged. Occasionally confused. The first applies to things that are built cheaply and without regard to quality. The second describes things made in haste, with whatever materials are to hand, as a temporary or emergency measure.

Johns Hopkins (note 's' on both) is the name of the university and medical centre in Baltimore, Maryland.

join together, link together. The Bible and marriage ceremonies notwithstanding, *join together* is almost always tautological. Similarly *linked together*, even when written by as eminent an authority as C. T. Onions: 'The first members of a group linked together by one of the above conjunctions . . .' (in *Modern English Syntax*).

Joneses, keeping up with the. Not *Jones'* or *Jones's* or other occasional variants.

Jonson, Ben, not *Johnson*, for the dramatist and poet.

Juilliard School of Music, New York City. Note *Jui-*.

jury-rigged. See JERRY-BUILT, JURY-RIGGED.

just deserts, not *desserts*. The expression has nothing to do with the sweet course after dinner. It comes from the French for 'deserve', which may help you to remember that it has just one middle 's'.

K

Katharine's Docks, St, London. Note the unusual spelling of *Katharine*.

KCB stands for Knight Commander of the Order of the Bath. Note the second *the*.

keenness. 'There is a distinct lack of keeness in the Labour camp for the proposal' (*Daily Telegraph*). Make it *-nn-*. The misspelling is common, no doubt because of a mistaken analogy with *keenest*. But the double-'n' rule applies to all words ending in 'n' when *ness* is added: 'openness', 'suddenness', 'outspokenness', 'meanness' and so on.

Khrushchev, Nikita. Few errors make a publication look more careless than misspelling the name of a world leader, and fewer leaders' names have been misspelled more frequently or variously than that of the late Soviet leader Nikita Khrushchev. The *Sunday Times* once managed to misspell the name two ways in a single picture caption: 'De-Stalinisation and the Khrushev era' (caption heading); 'Kruschev (right) denounces Stalin at the 20th Party Conference' (caption text). Note that the surname has three 'h's.

kibbutz, kibitz. The first refers to Israeli communal settlements (plural *kibbutzim*). The second is to watch at cards or some other such activity, often in an interfering manner.

kibitz. See KIBBUTZ, KIBITZ.

kind. 'Those are the kind of numbers that easily solve the mystery . . .' (*New York Daily News*). *Kind* and *kinds* and their antecedents should always enjoy what grammarians call concord. Just as we say 'this hat' but 'those hats', so the writer above should have said, 'Those are the kinds of numbers' or 'This is the kind of number'. Shakespeare, for what it is worth, didn't always observe the distinction. In *King Lear* he wrote: 'These kind of knaves'.

kindergarten, but *kindergartner*. Not *-gartener*.

Kingsford-Smith (hyphen) for the airport in Sydney, but *Sir Charles Kingsford Smith* (no hyphen) for the aviator after whom it was named.

kitemark (one word, lower case). It is the logo of the British Standards Institution indicating that a product has been approved as safe.

kith and kin. Your *kin* are your relatives. Your *kith* are your relatives and acquaintances. Individually the words are antiquated. Together they are hackneyed.

Kitts-Nevis, St, is the common name for the Caribbean state formally known as the Federation of St Christopher and Nevis.

Kmart for the American stores group but *Wal-Mart* for its rival.

knot. 'The yacht was doing about nine knots an hour, according to Mr Starr' (*The New York Times*). Because *knot* means nautical miles an hour, the time element is implicit in it. The sentence is telling us that the yacht was progressing at nine nautical miles an hour an hour. Either delete 'an hour' or change *knots* to 'nautical miles'.

koala bears is wrong. Koalas are marsupials and have no relation to bears. Just call them koalas.

krona, krone. The currencies of the Scandinavian nations cause occasional confusion, as in this *Times* headline: 'Sweden devalues kroner by 10 per cent'. The Swedes call it a *krona* (plural *kronor*). In Denmark and Norway it is a *krone* (plural *kroner*). In Iceland, it is also a *krona*, but the plural is *kronur*.

krone. See KRONA, KRONE.

Krugerrand. Occasionally misspelled, as here: 'The premium on Krugerands was just over 3 per cent' (*Guardian*). Note *-rr-*.

kudos. 'He did not feel he had received the kudos that were his due' (*Washington Post*). *Kudos*, a Greek word meaning fame or glory, is singular. Thus it should be 'the kudos that was his due'. There is no such thing, incidentally, as one kudo.

L

lackadaisical for something done without enthusiasm. Not *lacks-*.

La Guardia Airport, New York.

languid, limpid. Not to be confused. *Limpid* means clear, calm, untroubled ('a limpid stream'). It has nothing to do with being limp or listless – meanings that are covered by *languid*.

last, latest. Various authorities have issued various strictures against using *last* when you mean *latest*. Clearly, *last* should not be used when it might be misinterpreted, as in 'the last episode of the television series' when you mean the most recent but not the final one. However, it should also be noted that *last* in the sense of *latest* has a certain force of idiom behind it, and when ambiguity is unlikely (as in 'He spoke about it often during the last presidential campaign') a reasonable measure of latitude should be granted.

latest. See LAST, LATEST.

latter. See FORMER, LATTER.

laudable, laudatory. Occasionally confused. *Laudable* means deserving praise. *Laudatory* means expressing praise.

laudatory. See LAUDABLE, LAUDATORY.

lawful, legal. In many contexts the words can be used interchangeably, but not always. *Lawful* means permissible under the law ('lawful behaviour', 'lawful protest'). *Legal* has that meaning plus the additional sense of 'relating to the law', as in legal system or legal profession.

lay, lie. 'Laying on his back, Dalton used a long exposure of two seconds so as to achieve maximum depth of field' (*Photography* magazine). Unless Dalton was producing eggs, he was lying on his back. *Lay* and *lie*, in all their manifestations, are a constant source of errors. There are no simple rules for dealing with them. You must either commit their various forms to memory or avoid them altogether. The forms are:

	lay	*lie*
Present:	I lay the book on the table.	I lie down; I am lying down.
Past:	Yesterday I laid the book on the table.	Last night I lay down to sleep.
Present perfect:	I have already laid the book on the table.	I have lain in bed all day.

The most common type of error is to say: 'If you're not feeling well, go upstairs and lay down'. It should be 'lie down'.

lead, led. Confusion between the two is astonishingly – and really inexcusably – common, as here: 'The programme in Tissue Engineering will be lead by Professor Tim Hardingham, Manchester and Professor David Williams, Liverpool' (*New Scientist* advertisement from the University of Manchester and the University of Liverpool). The past tense spelling of the verb *lead* is *led*. It is also worth mentioning in passing that 'Manchester' in the example just cited should have a comma after it as well as before.

lectern, podium, dais, rostrum. The first two are frequently confused. A lectern is the stand on which a speaker places his notes. A podium is the raised platform on which he and the lectern stand. A podium can hold only one person. A platform for several people is a dais. A rostrum is any platform; it may be designed for one speaker or for several.

led. See LEAD, LED.

legal. See LAWFUL, LEGAL.

legend, legendary. Lytton Strachey once described Florence Nightingale as 'a living legend in her own lifetime' (as opposed, apparently, to a dead legend in her own lifetime) and thereby created a cliché that we could well do without. Properly, a legend is a story that may have some basis in fact, but is mostly fanciful. King Arthur and Robin Hood are legendary figures. The term can fairly be extended to those people or things whose fame is such as to inspire myths (Marilyn Monroe, Don Bradman, Rolls-Royces), but the word is often used much too loosely, as here: 'Doctors call it Munchhausen's syndrome, after the legendary ... Baron Hieronymous Karl Friedrich von Munchhausen, who spun fantastic and exaggerated stories about his experiences as a German cavalry officer ...' (*The New York Times*). To attach the word to a man whose fame exists almost exclusively within medical circles is to use it much too casually.

legendary. See LEGEND, LEGENDARY.

Leiden, Leyden. The first is the usual spelling for the Dutch town, the second for the scientific instrument known as a Leyden jar.

lend, loan. *Loan* as a verb ('He loaned me some money') is now more or less standard in America and is found increasingly in Britain, as here: 'They have agreed to loan the fund more than $4,000 million' (*The Times*). However, most British authorities and at least two leading American ones (Bernstein and *The American Heritage Dictionary*) urge that the usage be resisted. The Evanses, on the other hand, find *loan* as a verb entirely unobjectionable, pointing out that it has been so used for 800 years. Nor, they add, is it a sloppy Americanism, as is sometimes suggested; it appeared in an Act of Parliament as long ago as 1542.

less. See FEWER, LESS.

level, mark are often pointlessly employed. 'Share prices once again fell below the 600 level' (*Guardian*) says no more than 'fell below 600'. Similarly *mark*, as in 'This year's attendances have been hovering around the 25,000 mark' (*Sunday Times*). Make it 'hovering around 25,000'.

Leyden. See LEIDEN, LEYDEN.

Lhasa for the capital of Tibet, but *Lhaso apso* for the breed of dog.

liable, likely, apt, prone. All four indicate probability, but they carry distinctions worth noting. *Apt* is better reserved for general probabilities ('It is apt to snow in January') and *likely* for specific ones ('It is likely to snow today'). *Liable* and *prone* are better used to indicate a probability arising as a regrettable consequence: 'People who drink too much are prone to heart disease'; 'If you don't pay your taxes, you are liable to get caught'. A few older usage guides suggest that *prone* should apply only to people, but that seems to be an archaic view; the 1982 *Concise Oxford Dictionary*, for instance, cites 'strike-prone industries' as an acceptable usage.

A separate problem with *likely*, more common in America than elsewhere, is seen in this sentence: 'Cable experts say the agreement will likely strengthen the company's position' (*Washington Post*). When used as an adverb, *likely* needs to be accompanied by one of four helping words: 'very', 'quite', 'more' or 'most'. Thus the sentence should say 'will very likely strengthen'. A greater improvement still would be to recast and tighten the phrase entirely: 'Cable experts say the agreement is likely to strengthen the company's position'. (See also INCLINE.)

libel, slander. Although nearly all dictionaries define *libel* merely as a statement that defames or damages a person's reputation, it is worth remembering that it must do so unfairly or inaccurately. It is the wrongness of a contention that makes it libellous, not the harshness of it. Nor is it possible, strictly speaking, to libel the dead, so the term was used loosely here: 'The author's breezy assertion that he [Thomas Jefferson] fathered a child by his slave Sally Hemings is regarded by many in the society as a gross and terrible libel' (*Guardian*). Although a libel usually takes the form of a written utterance, drawings and other visual depictions may also be libellous. In all cases, a libel must be published (the word comes from the Latin *libellus*, meaning 'little book'). When defamatory remarks are merely spoken, the term to describe the action is *slander*.

licence, license. In British usage the first is the noun, the second the verb ('a licence to sell wines and spirits', but 'licensed premises'). In America, *license* is the spelling for both noun and verb. In British usage, the same pattern applies to several other noun/verb pairings, notably practice/practise, advice/advise, device/devise and prophecy/prophesy.

license. See LICENCE, LICENSE.

lie. See LAY, LIE.

Liechtenstein. Misspelled much too often, as here: 'The inspectors are interested also in the considerable amount of unsolicited purchases of Guinness shares coming from Swiss and Lichtenstein-based institutions' (*The Times*).

lifelong. 'Jesse Bishop was a lifelong drug addict who had spent 20 of his 46 years in prison' (*Guardian*). You might be a lifelong resident of New York or a lifelong church-goer or, at a stretch, a lifelong lover of music. But unless the unfortunate Mr Bishop had turned to drugs at a remarkably early age, *lifelong* is much too literal a word to describe his addiction.

lighted, lit. Either is correct. *Lighted*, however, is more usual when the word is being used as an adjective ('a lighted torch').

light years. 'So protracted have the discussions been that their progress should almost be measured not in years but in light years' (*Guardian*). Though the intention above was obviously facetious, it is as well to remember that light years are a measure of distance, not time. In temporal terms, one earth year and one light year are the same.

like, as. Problems often arise in choosing between *like* and *as*. Here are two examples, both from *The New York Times* and both wrong: 'Advertising agencies may appear as [make it *like*] homespun enterprises to the American public . . .'; 'On the surface it looks like [*as if*] all of the parties are preparing for serious bargaining'.

On the face of it, the rule is simple: *as* and *as if* are always followed by a verb; *like* never is. Therefore you would say, 'He plays tennis like an expert' (no verb after *like*), but, 'He plays tennis as if his life depended on it' (verb *depended*).

Although that is the rule, there may be times when you wish to suspend it. Except in the most formal writing, sentences like the one you are now reading and the two that follow should not be considered objectionable: 'She looks just like her mother used to'; 'He can't dance like he used to'. There is also one apparent inconsistency in the rule in that *like* may be used when it comes between 'feel' and an *-ing* verb: 'He felt like walking'; 'I feel like going abroad this year'.

A separate problem with *like* is that it often leads writers to make false comparisons, as here: 'Like the Prime Minister, his opposition to increased public spending is fierce' (*Daily Telegraph*). The writer has inadvertently likened 'Prime Minister' to 'opposition'. In order to liken person with person, the sentence needs to be recast: 'Like the Prime Minister, he is fiercely opposed to increased public spending', or words to that effect.

likely. See LIABLE, LIKELY, APT, PRONE.

Limbourg, Limburg. The first is a province of Belgium, the second a province of The Netherlands. The cheese is Limburg or Limburger.

limited means constrained, set within bounds. Unless there is the idea of a limit being imposed, the word is better avoided. It is reasonable enough to say that a special offer is available for a limited time, but to write, 'There was a limited demand for tickets' (*Daily Mail*) is absurd when what is meant is that fewer customers than had been hoped showed up.

limpid. See LANGUID, LIMPID.

lingua franca. See JARGON, ARGOT, LINGUA FRANCA.

link together. See JOIN TOGETHER, LINK TOGETHER.

lion's share is better avoided unless there is some suggestion of a greedy or selfish accumulation, a sense not intended here: 'The Territory, which controls the lion's share of Australia's high-grade uranium reserves . . .' (*Australian*). It is also, of course, a cliché. Why not say 'most' or 'the larger part' or whatever is appropriate?

liquefaction. See LIQUEFY, LIQUEFACTION.

liquefy, liquefaction. Both are commonly misspelled, as in this example: 'Indonesia intends to double its exports of liquified gas to Japan' (*The Times*).

lira, lire. '30,000 lira buy at least 30,000 glorious calories at all-you-can-eatery' (*Chicago Tribune* headline). The plura of *lira* is *lire*. A second problem with the headline is that sums of money are normally treated as singular. Thus it should be '30,000 lire buys'. The abbreviation for *lira*, incidentally, is *lit*.

lire. See LIRA, LIRE.

lit. See LIGHTED, LIT.

literally. All too often used as a kind of disclaimer by writers who mean, literally, the opposite of what they are saying. The result is generally excruciating: 'Hetzel was literally born with a butcher's knife in his mouth' (*Chicago Tribune*); 'After a slow start, they literally sliced up the Wildcats with their stunning last-half onslaught' (*San Francisco Chronicle*); 'Our eyes were literally pinned to the curtains' (cited by Fowler).

It should not need saying, but if you don't wish to be taken literally, don't use *literally*. The word means actually, not figuratively. It is acceptable only when it serves to show that an expression usually used figuratively is to be taken at its word, as in: 'He literally died laughing'.

livid. Originally *livid* indicated a bluish, leaden shade of the sort associated with bruising. It has since been extended to mean furious and argumentative, and in that sense is now well established. But the word has nothing to do with redness, as is often assumed, or with brightness, as was apparently thought here: 'For the sun room she chose a bold, almost livid, array of patterns and textures' (*Chicago Tribune*). Unless the sun room was decorated in a dullish blue, the word the writer wanted was 'vivid'.

Lloyd George, David (no hyphen) for the British Prime Minister, but *Earl Lloyd-George of Dwyfor* (hyphen) for his title as a peer.

Lloyds TSB Bank (no apos.), but *Lloyd's of London* (apos.) for the insurers.

loan. See LEND, LOAN.

loath, loathe. The first is an adjective that means reluctant, the second a verb that means to despise.

loathe. See LOATH, LOATHE.

local residents. 'The proposals have upset many local residents' (*Guardian*). Residents generally are local.

Longchamp, not *-champs*, for the French racecourse.

Love's Labour's Lost for the play by Shakespeare.

Luxembourg, Luxemburg. *Luxemburg* is an anglicized spelling of the French *Luxembourg*. One or two arbiters of usage, notably *The Oxford Dictionary for Writers and Editors*, prescribe *Luxemburg* for the country and the province in Belgium, and *Luxembourg* for the palace and gardens in Paris. But nearly all other authorities opt (sensibly, in my view) for consistency with *Luxembourg* throughout. The German political activist was Rosa Luxemburg.

Luxemburg. See LUXEMBOURG, LUXEMBURG.

luxuriant, luxurious. The words are not interchangeable, though the meanings sometimes overlap. *Luxuriant* indicates profusion ('luxuriant hair'). *Luxurious* means sumptuous and expensive ('a luxurious house'). A luxuriant carpet is a shaggy one; a luxurious carpet is an expensive one.

luxurious. See LUXURIANT, LUXURIOUS.

M

Mac, Mc, M'. In British usage all such words are treated as if they were spelled *Mac* when determining alphabetical order. Thus 'McGuire' would precede 'Mason'. In the US the alphabetical order of the letters is followed literally, and 'Mason' would precede 'McGuire'.

McDonald's (note apos.) for the American fast-food chain. It is too ubiquitous to be misspelled as often as it is. The company is the McDonald's Corporation.

McDonnell Douglas Corporation (now part of Boeing) but *Macdonnell Ranges* in Australia.

Magdalen College, Oxford, but *Magdalene College*, Cambridge.

magnum opus, opus magnum. The first is an author's principal work; the second is a great work.

major, as in a 'major initiative', 'major scandal', 'major road improvement' and so on, remains a severely overworked word, and thus brings a kind of tofu quality to much writing, giving it bulk but little additional flavour. Nearly always it is worth the effort of trying to think of a more precise or expressive term.

majority, like *major*, has been wearied by overuse, particularly in the expression 'the vast majority of', as in these three examples, all from authorities: 'The vast majority of conditional sentences . . .' (Partridge); 'In the vast majority of instances . . .' (Bernstein); 'The vast majority of such mistakes . . .' (Fowler). Even when written by the most discriminating writers, 'the vast majority of' seldom says more in four words than 'most' says in one.

Majority should be reserved for describing the larger of two clearly divisible things, as in 'A majority of the members voted for the resolution'. But even then a more specific description is usually better: '52 per cent', 'almost two thirds', 'more than 70 per cent', etc. When there is no sense of a clear contrast with a minority (as in 'The majority of his spare time was spent reading'), *majority* is always better avoided.

maleficence, malfeasance. The first means a propensity to cause hurt or harm. The second is a legal term describing wrongdoing.

malfeasance. See MALEFICENCE, MALFEASANCE.

Malory, Sir Thomas, for the fifteenth-century author (*Le Morte d'Arthur*) but *George Mallory* for the Everest explorer.

Manila for the capital of the Philippines. The paper and envelopes, etc., are usually spelled lower case: *manila*.

manner born, to the. Not *manor*. The expression is from *Hamlet*.

mantel, mantle. The first is the usual spelling for the frame around a fireplace (Burchfield insists upon it), the second for all other senses. Note also the spellings of the associated words *mantelshelf* and *mantelpiece*.

mantle. See MANTEL, MANTLE.

marginal is unobjectionable when used to describe something falling near a lower limit ('a marginal profit'). But it is a lame choice when all you mean is small or slight, as was the case here: 'There has been a marginal improvement in relations between police and blacks in the community' (*Guardian*).

It is also worth noting that *margin* denotes the difference between two quantities, not their range. Thus if Bradford City were to beat Manchester United 7–2 (and one can always hope), Bradford City have won by a margin of five. They did not have a margin of 7–2 or a 7–2 margin.

mark. See LEVEL, MARK.

Mary Celeste. See CELESTE, MARY.

masterful, masterly. Most authorities continue to insist that we observe a distinction between these two – namely that *masterly* should apply to that which is adroit and expert and *masterful* to that which is imperious and domineering. So in the following quotation *masterly* would have been the better word: 'Leroy (Satchel) Paige, a masterful pitcher and baseball showman . . .' (*Washington Post*). Useful as the distinction might be, it has to be noted that no leading dictionary insists on it and most don't even indicate that such a distinction exists. Moreover, it must be conceded that *masterly* often makes a clumsy adverb. Although it is grammatically correct to write, 'He swims masterly' or even 'He swims masterlily', few writers would be content to do so. *Masterly* should perhaps be your first choice when you mean in the manner of a master, but to insist on it at the expense of euphony or clarity is overfussy and probably indefensible.

masterly. See MASTERFUL, MASTERLY.

material. See GERMANE, RELEVANT, MATERIAL.

materialize is usually no more than a somewhat pompous synonym for 'occur', 'develop' or 'happen'. If the urge to use it is irresistible, at least try to ensure that it is not qualifying the wrong noun, as it was here: 'Hopes of an improvement in the second half of the year have not materialized' (*The Times*). The hopes had not been realized; what had not materialized was the improvement.

Maudsley Hospital, London. Not *Maude-*.

Mauretania, Mauritania. The first is the spelling for the ancient African country and two famous Cunard ships. The second is the spelling of the modern-day African country formally known as the Islamic Republic of Mauritania.

Mauritania. See MAURETANIA, MAURITANIA.

may. See CAN, MAY.

may well be. This expression frequently signals that what follows is little more than a guess, as in this curiously cautious statement from a saleroom story in *The Times*: 'On July 3, Christies will be offering a selection of Leonardos, Mantegnas, Raphaels, Parmigianinos, Rembrandts and van Dykes in what may well be the most valuable single property sale of recent times'. The London auction house, incidentally, is Christie's, with an apostrophe. (See also VAN DYCK, VANDYKE.)

me. See I, ME.

mean, median, midrange, mode. In British usage, the *mean* is the sum of all the numbers in a sample divided by the number of numbers. It has the same meaning as 'average'. The *median* is the middle number of an array of numbers arranged in order of magnitude. The *midrange* is the middle point between the smallest and largest numbers. The *mode* is the most commonly occurring number in a sample of numbers.

Those are the bald definitions, but it should be noted that many American dictionaries give definitions that conflict with the above. *The American Heritage Dictionary*, for instance, defines *mean* not as the average of a series of numbers but as the middle point in a series, quite a different thing. Clearly the scope for confusion is profound. Bearing in mind that terms like *mean* and *median* are at best vaguely understood by the general reader, your most prudent course of action is to use them extremely sparingly in anything other than technical writing.

media is a plural. There really is no excuse for treating it otherwise, yet increasingly it appears as a singular even in the most conservative and careful publications, as in this example from the *New Yorker*: 'One reporter, the *Wall Street Journal*'s Nicholas Kulish, dashed off a petition . . . saying that if the media was barred from the counting room they were prepared to go to court'.

median. See MEAN, MEDIAN, MIDRANGE, MODE.

mediate. See ARBITRATE, MEDIATE.

meet. See METE, MEET.

melamine for the type of plastic. It is not capitalized.

men's, women's. However eagerly department stores and the like may strive to dispense with punctuation in their signs (writing 'Mens Clothing' or 'Womens Department'), the practice is subliterate and to be avoided in any serious writing. Equally incorrect, if slightly less common, is placing the apostrophe after the 's' (e.g., 'mens' hats', 'womens' facials'). However, note that the apostrophe is discarded in the compounds 'menswear' and 'womenswear'. (See also CHILDREN'S; POSSESSIVES.)

Messerschmitt, not *-schmidt*, for the type of aircraft.

metal, mettle. For all his lexicographical genius, Samuel Johnson was not always the most consistent of spellers. It is thanks to him that we have such discordant pairs as 'deign' but 'disdain' and 'deceit' but 'receipt', among many others. With *metal* and *mettle*, however, his inconsistency of spelling was by design. Though both come from the Greek *metallon* (meaning 'a mine') and, before Johnson's time, were often spelled the same, he thought it would be useful to distinguish them. Thus *metal* is the spelling reserved for chemical elements such as gold and copper, and *mettle* for contexts describing courage or spirit. A common misspelling is seen here: 'Market conditions have put the hoteliers on their metal' (*Observer*).

metaphor, simile. Both are figures of speech in which two things are compared. A *simile* likens one thing to another, dissimilar one: 'He ran like the wind'; 'She took to racing as a duck takes to water'. A *metaphor*, on the other hand, acts as if the two compared things are identical and substitutes one for the other. Comparing the beginning of time to the beginning of a day, for instance, produces the metaphor 'the dawn of time'.

Enough has been written on the perils of mixed metaphors that it probably requires no more comment than to say that constructions such as the following are profoundly undesirable: 'This is a virgin field pregnant with possibilities' (cited by Fowler); 'Yet the President has backed him to the hilt every time the chips were down' (cited by Bernstein). The shortcoming of such sentences is not so much that they mix metaphors as that they mix clichés. When neither of the metaphors in a sentence is hackneyed, you might just get away with it – as Shakespeare clearly did when he wrote, 'Or to take arms against a sea of troubles'.

It should also be noted that it isn't necessary to have two metaphors to botch a sentence. One will do if it is sufficiently inappropriate, as it was here: 'Indiana, ranked the No. 1 swimming power in the nation, walked away with the Big Ten championships tonight' (Associated Press).

mete, meet. The first means to allot; the second means suitable. One metes out punishment but a fitting punishment is meet.

meteor, meteorite, meteoroid. *Meteoroids* are pieces of galactic debris floating through space. If they enter Earth's atmosphere as shooting stars, they are *meteors*. If they survive the fall to Earth, they are *meteorites*.

meteorite. See METEOR, METEORITE, METEOROID.

meteoroid. See METEOR, METEORITE, METEOROID.

meticulous. 'The story has been published in meticulously researched weekly parts . . .' (*Observer*). Several usage books, though fewer and fewer dictionaries, insist that the word does not mean merely very careful, but rather excessively so. Correctly used, it has a pejorative tone. The word today is so often misused by respected writers (the example above comes from Germaine Greer) that to object is itself perhaps a somewhat meticulous act. Still, unless you mean to convey a negative quality, it is usually better to use 'scrupulous', 'careful', 'painstaking' or some other synonym.

mettle. See METAL, METTLE.

Middlesbrough. Probably the most misspelled community name in Britain. Note that it is *-brough*, not *-borough*.

midrange. See MEAN, MEDIAN, MIDRANGE, MODE.

militate, mitigate. Often confused. To militate is to operate against or, much more rarely, for something: 'The news of the scandal militated against his election prospects'. To mitigate means to assuage, soften, make more endurable: 'His apology mitigated the insult'. *Mitigate against* often appears and is always wrong.

millepede. Not *milli-*.

minimize, strictly speaking, does not mean merely to play down or soften. It means to reduce to an absolute minimum.

minuscule. Frequently misspelled, as here: 'It is a market which was miniscule only five years ago' (*Guardian*). Think of *minus*, not *mini*.

minute detail. *Minute* in this expression is almost always redundant. 'The cube will be split into little pieces and its components examined in minute detail' (*Sunday Times*). Delete *minute*.

mischievous. All too commonly misspelled: '"All lawyers are really failed actors", says Ackland mischieviously' (*Independent*); 'He accused Harman of making misleading statements bordering on the mischievious after she claimed that drugs for patients would be cash-limited' (*Independent*). The words are *mischievously* and *mischievous*.

mishap. Generally, the word should suggest no more than a not very serious accident, which would rule out this headline: '30 die in mishap' (*The Times*). It isn't possible to say at what point exactly the word becomes inadequate to describe a misfortune, but it is unlikely to be any event involving multiple fatalities.

misogamist, misogynist. The first hates marriage, the second hates women.

misogynist. See MISOGAMIST, MISOGYNIST.

misspell. If there is one word that you don't wish in print to misspell, it is this one. Note *-ss-*.

mitigate. See MILITATE, MITIGATE.

mode. See MEAN, MEDIAN, MIDRANGE, MODE.

modus vivendi. Although *modus vivendi* is frequently used to mean 'way of life' (its literal meaning), a few of the more conservative authorities maintain that it should describe only a truce between parties pending settlement of their disagreement. The best way to avoid offending the learned or perplexing the ignorant is to find an English equivalent.

Monégasque for a person or thing from Monaco. Note that it is not *Mona-*.

mongooses is the plural of mongoose. The word is of Indian origin and has no relation to the English goose.

mononucleosis is the American term for the illness known in Britain and elsewhere as glandular fever.

more than and similar expressions such as *greater than* and *less than* call for some care when being positioned in sentences – at least more than was exercised here: 'It is a more than 200 per cent increase on the 15 million square feet planned in 1984' (*The Times*). The construction would be less ungainly as 'It is an increase of more than 200 per cent on the . . .'

moribund. 'Problems in the still-moribund oil tanker business mean there is little sign of recovery on the horizon' (*The Times*). *Moribund* does not mean troubled or struggling, as was intended above and frequently elsewhere. It means dying, on the point of death.

mortar, in the context of weaponry, is the launching device, not the explosive projectiles. It is generally better, and sometimes necessary, to write that troops fired *mortar rounds* (or bombs or shells, etc.) rather than simply that they fired *mortars*.

motiveless. 'French police have intensified their search for the killer in the motiveless murder of a Parisian housewife and her three children yesterday' (*The Times*). *Motiveless* is a careless word, and under English law a potentially dangerous one, in many contexts. Who is to say at an early stage of an investigation that a murder was committed without motive? At least make it 'apparently motiveless'.

Mount St Helens. See HELENS, ST.

mucous, mucus. The first is the adjectival form, the second the noun form. Thus *mucus* is the substance secreted by the *mucous* membranes.

mucus. See MUCOUS, MUCUS.

multilateral. See UNILATERAL, BILATERAL, MULTILATERAL.

munch. 'The most coveted invitation on a Sunday in Washington is to the Lombardi Room ... where pols, power brokers and media biggies munch hot dogs' (*The New York Times*). Most dictionaries define *munch* as to eat with a crunching sound, so it is better not to apply it to soft, noiseless food like hot dogs.

Muscovite. 'Moscovites in shock as queues vanish' (*Sunday Times*). People from Moscow are Muscovites, with a 'u', after the ancient principality of Muscovy.

'Music hath charms to soothe a savage breast' is the correct quotation from the 1697 Congreve play *The Mourning Bride*. It is not 'the savage breast' or 'a savage beast' or any of the other variants sometimes attributed to it.

mutual, common. Most authorities continue to insist, with varying degrees of conviction, that *mutual* should be reserved for describing reciprocal relationships between two or more things and not loosely applied to those things shared in common. Thus, if you and I like each other, we have a mutual friendship. But if you and I both like Shakespeare, we have a common admiration. The use of *mutual* in the sense of *common* has been with us since the sixteenth century and was given a notable boost in the nineteenth with the appearance of the Dickens novel *Our Mutual Friend*. Most authorities accept it when *common* might be interpreted as a denigration, but even so in its looser sense the word is generally better avoided. It is, at all events, more often than not superfluous, as here: 'They hope to arrange a mutual exchange of prisoners' (*Daily Telegraph*). An exchange of anything can hardly be other than mutual.

Muzak for the piped music associated with hotel lifts and the like. Note the initial cap.

myself. Except when it is used for emphasis ('I'll do it myself') or reflexively ('I cut myself while shaving') *myself* is almost always timorous and inapt. In the following two examples, the better word is inserted in brackets: 'Give it to John or myself [me]'; 'My wife and myself [I] would just like to say . . .'.

myth. See FABLE, PARABLE, ALLEGORY, MYTH.

N

nation. See COUNTRY, NATION.

National Institutes of Health, US. Note that *Institutes* is plural.

naught, nought. The first means 'nothing', as in 'His efforts came to naught'. The second is the figure zero. The game is noughts and crosses (known in the US as tick-tack-toe).

nauseous. 'Martinez left early, complaining that he felt nauseous' (*Newsweek*). Make it *nauseated*. *Nauseous* is an adjective describing something that causes nausea ('a nauseous substance'). As Bernstein once neatly put it, people who are nauseated are no more nauseous than people who are poisoned are poisonous.

naval, navel. The first pertains to a navy and its possessions or operations, the second to belly buttons and like-shaped objects. The oranges are *navel*.

navel. See NAVAL, NAVEL.

Neandertal increasingly is the preferred spelling for the extinct species of human, though the formal scientific rendering *Homo neanderthalensis* still generally keeps the *-thal* spelling. Neanderthal man, as a term for the species, is both sexist and old-fashioned.

near disaster. 'His quick thinking saved an RAF jet pilot from a near disaster' (*The Times*). Not quite. The pilot was saved from a disaster. A near disaster is what he had.

neat's-foot oil, a substance used to treat leather, is a term that seldom appears these days, but is almost always misspelled in one way or another when it does appear.

nebula. The plural can be either *nebulae* or *nebulas*.

needless to say is a harmless enough expression, but it often draws attention to the fact that you really didn't need to say it.

neither is a word that causes endless problems not only for writers but also sometimes for those who wish to guide them. *The Times Guide to English Style and Usage,* for instance, states flatly but perhaps just a touch blithely: 'neither takes a singular verb, eg, "neither Bert nor Fred has any idea"'. That is true enough, to be sure, for examples involving Bert and Fred or any other two singular items, but what if the items are plural? According to *The Times Guide,* we would have to write, 'Neither the men nor the women is dressed yet', which would be irregular to say the very least. And what if there is a mixture of singular and plural? Again, according to *The Times Guide,* we would have to write: 'Neither the farmer nor any of his fifty cows was in the field' and again we would be grammatically eccentric.

The rule, as you will gather, is slightly more complicated than is sometimes taught – but not so complicated that it should cause such persistent problems. Briefly put, in *neither . . . nor* constructions, the verb should always agree with the noun nearest it. Consider these two examples, both from the *Sunday Times* and both wrong: 'Neither De Niro nor his agent were available for comment'; 'Neither Gallagher nor Kensit were thought likely to attend'. In both cases, the nouns nearest the verb (respectively 'agent' and 'Kensit') are singular, so the verb should be singular. However, when the noun nearest the verb is plural, the verb should also be plural: 'Neither the Prime Minister nor his ministers were available for comment'.

When *neither* is used on its own without the *nor*, the verb should always be singular: 'Neither of the men was ready'; 'Neither of us is hungry'. In short, more often than not a singular verb is called for – but that singularity is by no means invariable. Try to remember that *neither* emphasizes the separateness of items. It doesn't add them together, at least not grammatically.

Finally, it should be noted that a *neither . . . or* combination is always wrong, as here: '[The] movie mixes horror with science fiction to make something that is fun as neither one thing or the other' (*The New York Times*). Make it *nor*. The following sentence makes the same error and the additional one of failing to provide a grammatical balance between the *neither* phrase and the *nor* phrase: 'Borrowing which allows a country to live beyond its means serves neither the interests of the borrower or the financial community' (*The Times*). Make it 'serves the interests of neither the borrower nor the financial community'. For a fuller discussion of the balancing problem, see BOTH . . . AND.

nemesis. 'Instead, the unions directed their wrath toward another nemesis, the European Community's Executive Commission . . .' (*Time* magazine). A nemesis (from Nemesis, the Greek goddess of vengeance) is not merely a rival or traditional enemy, but one who extracts retributive justice or is utterly unbeatable.

nerve-racking. Not *-wracking*. (See RACK, WRACK.)

new. 'New chairman named at Weir Group' (*Financial Times* headline); 'Medical briefing: the first in an occasional series on new developments in the sciences' (*Times* headline); 'The search for new breakthroughs seems to have spurred extra spending in recent years' (*Newsweek*). Far more often than not in journalism *new* is superfluous. The Weir Group would hardly be appointing an old chairman, nor scientists searching for old breakthroughs, nor *The Times*, let us hope, running a series on old developments in the sciences. In each instance it could be deleted without loss.

This rare double from *The New York Times* shows at a glance just how vacuous the word often is: 'New Boom for Florida Creates New Concerns'.

niceish is the spelling for something that is rather nice.

nincompoop. Not *nim-*.

no. See YES, NO.

nobody. See NUMBER (4).

noisome has nothing to do with noise or noisiness. It is related to annoy and means offensive or objectionable and is most often used to describe unpleasant smells.

none. The widely held belief that *none* must always be singular is a myth. Since Fowler, Bernstein, Howard, Gowers, Partridge, the Evanses, the Morrises, Follett, *The Oxford English Dictionary*, *The American Heritage*, *Random House* and *Webster's New World* dictionaries and many others have already made this point, I do not suppose that the addition of my own small voice to the chorus will make a great deal of difference.

Whether you treat *none* as a singular or a plural, you should at least be consistent throughout the sentence, as this writer was not: 'None of her friends, she says, would describe themselves as a feminist' (*Guardian*). Make it either 'would describe themselves as feminists' or 'would describe herself as a feminist'.

A more notable inconsistency, if only because it comes from a respected authority, is seen here: 'The total vocabulary of English is immense and runs to about half a million items. None of us as individuals, of course, knows more than a fairly limited number of these, and uses even less' (Quirk, *The Use of English*). 'None of us . . . uses even less'? The sentence appears to be telling us that nobody uses fewer words than he knows, which is unfortunately the opposite of what the author intended. It would be better if we made it 'and we use even less' – and better still if we made it 'and we use even fewer'.

non sequitur is the Latin for 'it does not follow' and means the combination of two or more statements that are jarringly unrelated, as in 'He was born in Liverpool and his shoes were brown'. Non sequiturs are most often encountered in American newspapers, where constructions such as the following are common: 'Slim, of medium height and with sharp features, Mr Smith's technical skills are combined with strong leadership qualities' (*The New York Times*). What, we might ask, do Mr Smith's height and features have to do with his leadership qualities? The answer, of course, is not a thing. When non sequiturs are not intrusive and annoying, they are often just absurd, as here: 'Dyson's catch of Clarke was unbelievable, the best catch I've seen. And the one before it was just as good' (*Sydney Daily Telegraph*, cited in *Punch*).

no one. See NUMBER (4).

normalcy is widely and wrongly condemned as an inelegant Americanism, often attributed to President Warren G. Harding, who promised voters 'a return to normalcy' in the 1920s. In fact, the word is much older and is British in origin. Although most dictionaries accept it as standard, it is still derided by many authorities, who suggest 'normality' instead.

not. Sometimes when writers invert the normal word order of a sentence to place greater emphasis on *not*, they present the reader with a false parenthesis. It is a fault to which even usage guides are sometimes prey, as here: 'Could not that lingua franca be, not Esperanto, Volupük, or even English, but humour?' (Simon, *Paradigms Lost*). As punctuated, 'not Esperanto, Volupük or even English' is parenthetical. But if we deleted it (as we should be able to do with all parenthetical expressions), the sentence would read: 'Could not that lingua franca be but humour?' The first comma is wrong and should be deleted. Except when the sentiment is pithy ('Death be not proud') such sentences are usually clumsy, which may account for the urge to embellish them with unnecessary punctuation.

A separate but common problem with *not* is seen in this

headline from *The Times*: 'Social class not spending determines exam results, survey shows'. When *not* is used to introduce a contrast, it must be preceded by a comma and have a concluding comma at the end of the phrase to signal to the reader the change of direction (the example above should read: 'Social class, not spending, determines exam results . . .'). Otherwise he is likely to try to attach the word to what has gone before it, as he would in a statement like 'Social class not a factor in exam results'. The problem is particularly prevalent in headlines, where small linking words are often omitted for the sake of brevity, but it also appears in text, as here: 'Responsibility for the misjudgement must be placed firmly at the feet of Mrs Thatcher not her ministers' (*Guardian*). The reader may be thrown off the scent for no more than an instant, but even that is an unjustifiable imposition. Insert a comma or an *and* after 'Thatcher'.

not all. 'For some time now tales have been circulating that all was not well in the Goldsmith empire' (*The Times*). What the writer really meant, of course, was that not all was well in the empire, not that everything was unwell. The authorities are curiously, and almost unanimously, tolerant on this point. The Evanses are actually rather vehement about it: 'Distinctions such as this, between *all is not* and *not all is*, appeal to a fictitious logic and seem to have been invented for the purposes of proving other people wrong. They are not good for much else'.

I'm afraid the authorities and I are at odds here – or, as the Evanses might put it, all of us don't agree. It seems to me difficult to justify a sentence that so blatantly contradicts what it is meant to say, especially when the solution is as simple a matter as moving the *not* back two places. Setting aside any considerations of grammatical tidiness and rectitude, if we accept the Evanses' position, how do we make ourselves clear when we really do mean that all isn't well? There are a few expressions that unquestionably have the weight of idiom behind them ('All is not lost', 'All that glisters is not gold'), but on the whole in careful writing I think the construction is better avoided. Certainly I wouldn't want to have to defend the New York clothing store that advertised: 'All items not on sale' (cited by William Safire in *The New York Times*).

Notes from Underground is the 1864 novel by Dostoevsky. Not *the Underground*.

not only . . . but also. See BOTH . . . AND.

not so much is often followed by *but* when the word should be *as*, as here: 'He was not so much a comic actor, consciously presenting an amusing part, but a real comedian' (J. B. Priestley, cited by Partridge). Make it 'as a real comedian'.

nought. See NAUGHT, NOUGHT.

Nullarbor Plain, Western Australia. Often misspelled *Nullabor*.

number. Errors of number – the failure to maintain agreement between the subject and verb in a sentence – are probably the most common grammatical fault in English and often the least excusable. In a language where so much is so complicated, the rule is gratifyingly simple: a singular subject takes a singular verb and a plural subject takes a plural verb. As Bernstein says, anyone who can distinguish between one and more than one shouldn't find that too sophisticated a challenge. Yet errors abound – even, as we shall see, among those who should know better. Many of the causes of errors are treated separately throughout the book, but five in particular are worth noting here:

1. *Errors involving 'and'.* When two nouns or pronouns joined by *and* form a compound subject, a plural verb is required. 'Impatience and anger in political and editorial circles has been sharply mounting . . .' (*Los Angeles Times*). Make it 'have'. 'She told the meeting that the disorder and despair of the Conservative Party was not self-evident' (*The Times*). Make it 'were'.

The error is especially common when the normal subject–verb order is reversed, as here: 'Why, you may ask, is correct speech and writing important, as long as the writing is clear?' (Simon, *Paradigms Lost*). Speech and writing 'are' important.

Simon might argue – indeed, he would have to – that 'speech' and 'writing' are so closely related that they form a single idea. When that is the case a singular verb is unobjectionable. But such exceptions are better kept for things that are routinely combined – fish and chips, ham and eggs, law and order, the long and the short of it, etc. – and even then a plural verb would not be wrong.

2. *Errors involving 'or'.* Whereas *and* draws diverse elements together, *or* keeps them separate. When all the elements are singular, the verb should be singular too. Thus this sentence is wrong: 'A nod, wink or even a discreet tug of the ear aren't [make it 'isn't'] going to be the only sign language at the auction . . .' (*Observer*). When all the elements are plural, the verb should be plural. When there is a mixture of singulars and plurals, the rule is to make the verb agree with the noun or pronoun nearest it. Consider: 'No photographs or television footage have been transmitted from the fleet for almost a week' (*The New York Times*). Because the nearest noun (footage) is singular, the verb should be 'has'. Had the two nouns been reversed, 'have' would have been correct.

The need to maintain agreement can sometimes lead to awkward constructions, particularly with pronouns. 'Is he or we wrong?' is grammatically perfect but perfectly awful. The solution would be to recast the sentence: 'Is he wrong or are we?'

A final point to note is that *or* influences not only the verb, but also subsequent nouns and pronouns. In the following sentence the correct forms are given in parentheses: 'While Paris, Mexico City, Hong Kong or Munich have (has) shown how their (its) underground systems (system) can become part of the pride of their (its) city . . .' (*Observer*). A better alternative with that sentence, however, would be to change the *or* to *and* and leave the rest of it as it is.

3. *Errors caused by failure to keep track of antecedents.* Few people, it sometimes seems, have shorter attention spans than the average writer. All too often he will confidently set out with

a plural or singular noun, become distracted by three or four intervening words and finish with a verb of the opposite number. Such was the case in each of the following (the correct forms are given in parentheses): 'Bank mortgages, which now account for most expensive property, is (are) not included in the figures . . .' (*The Times*); 'The pressure of living and working on board 24 hours a day have (has) led to some strained relationships' (*Observer*); 'The incident demonstrates the reluctance with which some requests for interviews with ministers and senior officials is (are) met' (*The Times*).

Occasionally the writer does not even have the excuse of intervening matter: 'Meet Allan and Sondra Gotlieb, whose official titles may cause glazed looks but whose frankness have made them among the most popular, and unusual, diplomats in Washington' (*The New York Times*). Frankness 'have'?

And sometimes the intervening matter is so clearly unconnected with the main clause that the error is startling – all the more so when it is committed by as careful a user as Philip Howard: 'Populist (and its generic class of politics, populism) have recently been adopted as vogue words in British politics . . .' (from *New Words for Old*). Make it 'has recently been adopted as a vogue word'. For a discussion, see PARENTHESES in the Appendix.

4. *Errors involving personal pronouns.* This is a common type and one that points up the inadequacies both of English and of those who use it. Consider. 'If someone is learning a language for their job . . .' (*Financial Times*). The problem is that the singular 'someone' and singular 'is' are being attached to the plural 'their'. Grammatically it is equivalent to saying 'No one were there' or 'They is studying French'.

The convention is to make the second pronoun 'his': 'If someone is learning a language for his job . . .'. The obvious shortcoming is that this slights women. To avoid offending either them or grammar, you could make it 'his or her job', which is often cumbersome, or you could recast the sentence with a plural subject: 'People who are learning a language for their job . . .'. I recommend recasting.

Too strict an application of the rule can result in incongruities – a point that evidently occurred to Philip Howard when he penned the following sentence in *Words Fail Me*: 'Nobody pretends any more (if they ever did) that economics is an exact science'. 'If they ever did' is strictly incorrect, but to change it to 'if he ever did' would unbalance the sense of the sentence. One way of preserving the grammar would be to make the subject plural: 'Few people pretend any more . . .'. Another would be to replace 'they' with a singular pronoun: 'Nobody pretends any more (if anyone ever did) that economics is an exact science'. These solutions are not perhaps entirely satisfactory – but then neither, I think, is a grammatical error.

Whichever tack you take, you should at least be consistent throughout the sentence. Here is one in which the writer went to some lengths to get his pronouns right before abruptly self-destructing just short of home: 'Anyone who does confess to being a Sedaka fan does so with the guarded reluctance of one edging out of the closet, fearing he or she will be made immediate targets of fun' (*Sunday Times*). It should be 'an immediate target of fun'.

5. *Errors involving the word 'number'*. There is frequent confusion over whether to use a plural or singular verb with the noun *number*. Both of the following examples come from the same issue of *The Times*. Both are wrong. 'Mr Isaacs said a substantial number of households was inhabited today not by the conventional family group, but by single tenants'; 'A small, but increasing number of individuals is apparently buying secondhand British Rail coaches'. There is an easy way out of the confusion. Always make it 'The number was . . .' but 'A number were . . .'. The same rule applies to TOTAL.

numbers in text. 'For more than a 1,000 years, the Venetians have laboured to preserve the delicate balance of their watery domain . . .' (*Independent*); 'Fugly has become the most impounded mutt in Australia with over a 100 convictions . . .' (*Independent*). When numbers to a power of ten such as these are written out, they mean 'one hundred', 'one thousand' and so on. Putting an indefinite article in front of them is to say in effect 'a one hundred convictions' or 'a one thousand years'. Make it 'a thousand years' or '1,000 years', or 'a hundred convictions' or '100 convictions', but don't combine the two.

numskull, not *numbskull*, is the preferred spelling in both Britain and America.

Nuremberg (German *Nürnberg*) for the Bavarian city. Not *-burg*.

O

oblivious. Fowler, Partridge and the *OED*, among others, long maintained that *oblivious* can mean only forgetful. You cannot properly be oblivious of something that you were not in the first place aware of. But in its broader sense of merely being unaware or impervious, *oblivious* is now accepted universally.

obsolescent. See OBSOLETE, OBSOLESCENT.

obsolete, obsolescent. Things that are no longer used or needed are *obsolete*. Things that are becoming obsolete are *obsolescent*.

obviate does not mean reduce or make more acceptable, as is often thought: 'A total redesign of the system should obviate complaints about its reliability' (*The Times*). It means to make unnecessary.

occur, take place. *Take place* is better reserved for scheduled events. When what is being described is accidental, *occur* is the better word, as it would have been here: 'The accident took place in driving rain' (*Guardian*).

oculist. See OPHTHALMOLOGIST, OCULIST, OPTOMETRIST, OPTICIAN.

off of is redundant. Write 'Get off the table', not 'Get off of the table'.

Oireachtas for the Irish legislature, consisting of the President and the two assemblies, the Dáil Éireann and the Seanad Éireann. It is pronounced *ur'-akh-tus*.

Old Peculier, not *Peculiar*, for the beer brewed by Theakston.

Olympic-sized swimming pool. '. . . and in fitting movie star fashion, the grounds include an Olympic-sized swimming pool' (*Mail on Sunday*). An official Olympics swimming pool is fifty metres long. Virtually no private person, even in Hollywood, owns a pool that large. The description is almost always a gross exaggeration.

Omar Khayyám is the correct spelling of the Persian poet and mathematician. Note *-yy-*.

on, upon. Although some journalists think there is, or ought to be, a distinction between these two, there isn't. The choice is sometimes dictated by idiom ('upon my word', 'on no account'), but in all other instances it is a matter of preference.

one. 'The makers claim that one in 14 people in the world are following the exploits of this new hero' (*Sunday Times*). In such constructions *one* should be singular. In effect the sentence is saying: 'Out of every 14 people in the world, one is following the exploits of this new hero'. A slightly trickier case appears here: 'An estimated one in three householders who are entitled to rebates are not claiming' (*The Times*). The first *are* is correct, but the second is wrong. Again, it may help to invert the sentence: 'Of those householders who are entitled to rate rebates, one in every three is not claiming'.

one another. See EACH OTHER, ONE ANOTHER.

one of the, one of those. The problem here is similar to that discussed under ONE above, but with the difference that here *one* does not govern the verb. Consider: 'Nott is actually one of those rare politicians who really doesn't mind what he says' (*Observer*). The operative word here is not *one* but *those*, as can be seen by inverting the sentence: 'Of those politicians who do not mind what they say, Nott is one'.

The mistake is a common one. Even Gowers made it when he revised Fowler's *Dictionary of Modern English Usage*: 'Prestige is one of the words that has had an experience opposite to that described in "Worsened Words"'. It should be 'have had'. Sixty pages earlier he called the error 'a frequent blunder'.

It should also be noted that *one of the* is very often verbose, as in these examples: 'One of the reasons for all the excitement . . .' (*Sunday Telegraph*); 'One of the members said he would almost certainly abstain' (*Guardian*). Better, generally, to make it 'one reason', 'one member' and so on.

one or more is plural. 'Inside each folder is one or more sheets of information' (cited by Bernstein) should be 'are one or more'.

only. In general, *only* ought to be attached to the word or phrase it is modifying and not set adrift, as here: 'The A Class bus only ran on Sundays' (*Observer*). Taken literally, the sentence suggests that on other days of the week the bus did something else – perhaps flew? The writer would better have said that the bus 'ran only on Sundays' or 'on Sundays only'.

Oftentimes clarity and idiom are better served by bringing *only* to a more forward position ('This will only take a minute', 'The victory can only be called a miracle'). And increasingly, it must be said, authorities are inclined towards leniency with regard to where *only* is permitted. Certainly it is always better to avoid an air of fussiness. But when, as in the example above, a simple repositioning puts the word in the right place without creating a distraction, there is no reason not to do it.

onto. See ON TO, ONTO.

on to, onto. Until the twentieth century *onto* as one word was almost unknown in both Britain and America, and its standing remains somewhat dubious in Britain. Many British authorities continue to insist that *on to* should be two words always or nearly always – which sometimes leads, it must be said, to a certain vagueness of explication. *The Times Guide to Style and Usage*, for instance, allows constructions such as 'he collapsed onto the floor', but otherwise insists that *onto* be used as one word 'as little as possible'. In America, the position is somewhat clearer. There, *onto* is used where the two elements function as a compound preposition ('He jumped onto the horse') and *on to* is used where *on* is an adverb ('We moved on to the next subject'). This, it will be noted, is essentially the position *The Times* is urging without actually saying so. In any case, I would submit that the American pattern of use is already rapidly becoming standard in Britain, which frankly in this instance is no bad thing.

openness. Note *-nn-*.

ophthalmologist, oculist, optometrist, optician. *Ophthalmologist* can frequently be seen misspelled. Note that it begins *oph-* and not *opth-* and that the first syllable is pronounced *off*, not *op*. Thus it is similar in pronunciation and spelling to *diphtheria*, *diphthong* and *naphtha*, all of which are also frequently misspelled and mispronounced.

Ophthalmologist and *oculist* both describe doctors who specialize in diseases of the eye. An *optometrist* is one who is trained to test eyes but is not a doctor. An *optician* is one who makes or sells corrective lenses.

opposite. See CONTRARY, CONVERSE, OPPOSITE, REVERSE.

opt, choose. Safire suggests that *opt* would be a more expressive word if we used it only to describe impulsive choices, and he is right. But it must be said that none of the leading dictionaries note or encourage such a distinction.

optician. See OPHTHALMOLOGIST, OCULIST, OPTOMETRIST, OPTICIAN.

optimistic, pessimistic. Strictly speaking, both words should be used to describe a general outlook rather than a specific view, particularly with regard to the inconsequential. 'He was optimistic that he would find the missing book' would be better as 'was hopeful' or 'was confident'.

optimum does not mean greatest or fastest or biggest, as is sometimes thought. It describes the point at which conflicting considerations are reconciled. The optimum flying speed of an aircraft, for instance, is the speed at which all the many variables that must be taken into account in flying – safety, comfort, fuel consumption and so on – are most nearly in harmony.

optometrist. See OPHTHALMOLOGIST, OCULIST, OPTOM-ETRIST, OPTICIAN.

opus magnum. See MAGNUM OPUS, OPUS MAGNUM.

or has the grammatical effect of emphasizing the separateness of items rather than adding them together. If a grammarian offers you an apple or a pear or a banana, he means that you may have one of them, not all three. When *or* links two or more singular items in a sentence, the verb must always be singular. 'It was not clear whether the President or Vice-president were within hearing range at the time' (*Chicago Tribune*) should be 'was within hearing range'. If that sounds stilted, you can flag the singularity by inserting 'either' ahead of the phrase ('It was not clear whether either the President or Vice-President was within hearing . . .') or, more simply still, you can change *or* to 'and', thus justifying the plural verb. For a full discussion, see NUMBER (2).

oral, verbal. 'The 1960 understanding . . . was a verbal under-standing that was never written down' (*The New York Times*). Because *oral* can apply only to the spoken word, it would have been a better choice here. *Verbal*, which can describe both spoken and written words, is more usefully employed to distinguish between words and gestures or between words and substance. In the example above, however, neither word is necessary. It would be enough to say, 'The 1960 understanding was never written down'.

ordinal numbers. See CARDINAL NUMBERS, ORDINAL NUMBERS.

orientate is not incorrect, but it has nothing to recommend it over the shorter and simpler *orient*.

originally is often needlessly inserted into sentences where it conveys no additional information, as here: 'The plans were originally drawn up as long ago as 1972' (*Observer*).

Orkney. The collection of Scottish islands is properly labelled Orkney or the Orkney Islands, but not *the Orkneys*. A native or resident is an Orcadian.

'Ours is not to reason why, ours is but to do or die' is often heard, but is wrong. The lines from Tennyson's 'The Charge of the Light Brigade' are 'Their's not to reason why, / Their's but to do and die'. Note that the closing words 'do and die' give the lines an entirely different sense. Finally, it should be noted that Tennyson's punctuation of 'theirs' is irregular. (See POSSESSIVES.)

over. The notion that *over* is incorrect for 'more than' (as in 'over 300 people were present at the rally') is a widely held superstition. The stricture has been traced to Ambrose Bierce's *Write It Right* (1909), a usage book teeming with quirky recommendations, most of which have since been discarded. There is no harm in preferring 'more than', but also no basis for insisting on it.

overly. 'I didn't wish to appear overly earnest, but I couldn't help but wonder what was in the box' (*Philadelphia Inquirer*). Making *over* into *overly* is a little like turning 'soon' into 'soonly'. Adding *-ly* does nothing for *over* that it could not already do. The practice in America generally is to attach *over* directly to the word it is modifying (overearnest, overalarmist); in Britain, hyphens are more usual (over-careful, over-eager).

overweening. Arrogant or presumptuous expectations are overweening ones. There is no word *overweaning*.

'Ozymandias' for the 1818 sonnet by Shelley. Not *Oxy-*.

P

paean, paeon, peon. A *paean* is a hymn or song of praise. A *paeon* is a metrical foot in classical poetry. A *peon* is a servant or peasant.

paeon. See PAEAN, PAEON, PEON.

pail, pale. The first is a small bucket; the second means lacking colour.

palaeology (US paleology), **palaeontology** (US paleontology). The first is the study of antiquities. The second is the study of fossils.

palaeontology. See PALAEOLOGY, PALAEONTOLOGY.

palate, palette, pallet. *Palate* has to do with the mouth and taste. *Palette* is the board used by artists. *Pallet* is a mattress, a machine part or the wooden platforms on which freight is stood.

pale. See PAIL, PALE.

palette. See PALATE, PALETTE, PALLET.

pallet. See PALATE, PALETTE, PALLET.

pallor. Not -*our*.

panacea is a universal remedy, a cure for all woes, and is not properly applied to a single shortcoming, as it was here: 'One of the best panaceas for the styling similarity of many modern cars seems to be the removal of the roof' (*Observer*).

parable. See FABLE, PARABLE, ALLEGORY, MYTH.

parlay, parley. The first is to use one gain to make another ('He parlayed his winnings by doubling his bet'). The second is a conference.

partially. See PARTLY, PARTIALLY.

partly, partially. Although they are often interchangeable, their meanings are slightly different. *Partially* means incompletely and *partly* means in part. 'The house was made partially of brick and partially of stone' would be better as 'partly of brick and partly of stone'.

past. Often a space-waster, as in this example: 'She has been a teacher at the school for the past 20 years' (*Independent*). In this sentence, and in countless others like it, 'the past' could be deleted without any loss of sense.

past history. 'The Tristan islanders talk of their past history with great pride' (*Sunday Times*). *Past* in this expression is hopelessly redundant, as it is in past records, past experience, past achievements and past precedents.

pastiche. 'This provided the occasion for a successful pastiche of that great Fonda film, Twelve Angry Men' (*The Times*). A pastiche is a work inspired by a variety of sources. The word the writer was groping for here was 'parody'.

patois. See DIALECT, PATOIS.

peaceable, peaceful. *Peaceful* means tranquil and serene. *Peaceable* is a disposition towards the state of peacefulness.

peaceful. See PEACEABLE, PEACEFUL.

pease pudding for the dish.

pedagogue. See PEDANT, PEDAGOGUE.

pedal, peddle. The first applies to devices or actions involving foot power – the pedal on a piano, to pedal a bicycle. The second is a verb only, meaning to sell goods in an informal or itinerant manner. In British usage, a person who peddles objects is traditionally termed a *pedlar*, but increasingly through American influence the spelling *peddler* has made inroads, particularly with the term *drug peddler*.

pedant, pedagogue. The two are synonyms. They describe someone who makes an ostentatious show of his learning or is dogmatically fussy about rules. Some dictionaries still give *pedagogue* as a synonym for teacher or educator, but its pejorative sense has effectively driven out the neutral one.

peddle. See PEDAL, PEDDLE.

peninsula. 'Genetic evidence published last year, however, suggested a second route along the south coast of the Arabian peninsular' (*Economist*). A narrow piece of land jutting into a body of water is a *peninsula*. *Peninsular* is the adjectival form, as in 'peninsular war' or 'peninsular campaign'.

penn'orth for 'a penny's worth'.

peon. See PAEAN, PAEON, PEON.

per. Many usage guides suggest, and a few insist, that Latinisms like *per* should be avoided when English phrases are available – that it is better to write 'ten tons a year' than 'ten tons per annum'. Some also suggest that it is better not to mix Latin and English, as in 'ten tons per year'. All that is reasonable enough in general, but I would suggest that when avoidance of the Latin would result in clumsy constructions such as 'output a man a year', you shouldn't hesitate to use *per*.

per cent, percentage point. There is an important distinction between the two words that is not always observed even on the financial pages. Consider the following example from the business section of *The Times*. Headline: 'US tax reform to cut top rate by 25%'. Story: 'US Senate and House officials have begun work on [a] tax reform bill which would cut the top rate for individuals from 50 per cent to an estimated 25 per cent'. In short, the tax rate is to fall by half and not, as the headline suggests, by a quarter.

Put another way, if interest rates are 10 per cent and they rise to 11 per cent, they have risen by one percentage point, but by 10 per cent in value. In everyday contexts this difference in meaning can often be overlooked. Even in financial circles people routinely talk about a 2 per cent rise in mortgage rates when strictly they mean a two-point rise. But in contexts in which the percentage rise is large and ambiguity is likely, the distinction can be critical.

Finally it should be noted that the American spelling is *percent*.

percentage, proportion. The words are used inexactly when the relationship between two numbers isn't specified. 'This drug has proved of much value in a percentage of cases' (cited by Gowers) tells us next to nothing. It could mean 2 per cent or 28 per cent or 92 per cent. Similarly, 'a ship of large proportions' would be better replaced by 'a ship of large dimensions' or simply 'a large ship'.

percentage point. See PER CENT, PERCENTAGE POINT.

perceptible. Not -*able*.

perchance, perforce. The first means possibly. The second means without choice.

perforce. See PERCHANCE, PERFORCE.

period of time. A curiously irresistible expression for many writers, as here: 'Marcos claimed that the seizures could be expected to continue for a considerable period of time' (*Sunday Times*). Make it either 'a considerable period' or 'a considerable time'. Both together are unnecessary.

perpetrate, perpetuate. Occasionally confused. To perpetrate is to commit or perform. To perpetuate is to prolong or, literally, to make perpetual. Jack the Ripper perpetrated a series of murders. Those who write about him perpetuate his notoriety.

perpetuate. See PERPETRATE, PERPETUATE.

perseverance. See PERSEVERE, PERSEVERANCE.

persevere, perseverance. Not -*ser*-.

personal, personally. When it is necessary to emphasize that a person is acting on his own rather than as a spokesman or that he is addressing people individually rather than collectively, *personal* and *personally* are unexceptionable. But usually the context makes that clear and the word is used without purpose, as it was here: 'Dr Leonard has decided to visit personally the Oklahoma parish which is the centre of the dispute . . .' (*Daily Telegraph*). He could hardly do otherwise. *Personal* in many other common terms – personal friend, personal opinion, personal favourite – is nearly always equally redundant.

personally. See PERSONAL, PERSONALLY.

perspicacity, perspicuity. *Perspicacity* means shrewdness and applies to people ('a perspicacious judge of character'). *Perspicuity* means easily understood and applies to things ('a perspicuous explanation'). In both cases, a simpler synonym – 'shrewd' for the first, 'clear' for the second, for example – is often advisable.

perspicuity. See PERSPICACITY, PERSPICUITY.

persuade. See CONVINCE, PERSUADE.

perturb. See DISTURB, PERTURB.

peruse. 'Those of us who have been idly perusing the latest flock of holiday brochures . . .' (*Guardian*). It is a losing battle no doubt, but perhaps worth pointing out that *peruse* does not mean to look over casually. It means to read or examine carefully.

pessimistic. See OPTIMISTIC, PESSIMISTIC.

Peterhouse, the Cambridge college, is never called *Peterhouse College*.

Phalange. See FALANGE, PHALANGE.

Philippines. Note one 'l', double 'p'. A person from the Philippines is a Filipino if male, a Filipina if female. Filipino is also the name of the national language.

phrasal verbs is a somewhat ungainly term for what is unquestionably one of the more versatile features of English – namely the ability to extend the meaning of verbs by attaching a particle to them. Thus in English we can *break up*, *break off*, *break down*, *break in* and *break into*, or *take to*, *take off*, *take in*, *take up*, *take down* or *take away*, among many others. Each expression conveys a shade of meaning that would not be possible without the particle. But this capacity to grace a verb with a tail sometimes leads writers to add a word where none is needed. Thus we get *head up*, *check out*, *lose out*, *cut back*, *trigger off*, *pay off* and countless others. Sometimes such combinations, though strictly unnecessary, gain the force of idiom (*stand up*, *sit down*, *beat up*), but often they are merely a sign of careless writing. In the following examples, the italicized words do nothing but consume space: 'Now the bureau proposes to sell *off* 280 acres . . .' (*Time* magazine); 'The time will be cut *down* to two hours within two years' (*Daily Telegraph*); 'A light snowfall did little to slow *down* the British advance' (*Sunday Times*).

pidgin. See CREOLE, PIDGIN.

Pittsburgh. No doubt because it is pronounced with a hard 'g', the name of the Pennsylvanian city is often misspelled by Britons, even occasionally when they have recently been there: 'But let me pass them by, for one, more pleasant, glance of a prison on the same plan which I afterwards saw at Pittsburg' (Dickens, *American Notes*).

pizzeria, not *pizza-,* for the place where pizzas are made.

place names. A common punctuation error with place names is seen in the following examples: 'Fourteen people were arrested after police stopped an illegal pay party at Portchester, Hampshire and three people were arrested at a similar event at Christchurch, Dorset' (*Independent*); 'More than 200 million notes have been produced at the Bank of England's printing works in Debden, Essex and about 2.5 million more will roll off the presses every day' (*Independent*). Commas are required after the county name as well as before it. The same applies to states, provinces, countries and so on when they follow the name of a town or city.

plan ahead. '[The] keys to success are to plan ahead, to choose manageable recipes and to cook in batches' (*The New York Times*). Always tautological. Would you plan behind?

plea, plead. 'Police in plea for more funds' (*Evening Standard* headline). The story beneath the headline described a routine request for more money. Unless there is a genuine sense of urgency, and at least a hint of submissive entreaty, *plea* almost always overstates the case. It is without argument a usefully compact headline word, but so are the more neutral words 'seek' and 'ask'. (See also GRIEF, GRIEVE.)

plead. See PLEA, PLEAD.

plenitude for the sense of abundance. Not *plenti-*.

pleonasm. See TAUTOLOGY, REDUNDANCY, PLEONASM, SOLECISM.

plethora is not merely a lot, it is an excessive amount, a superabundance. For a word that is often similarly misused, see SPATE.

plus. 'The end of the holiday season plus the fact that London banks remained closed were cited as factors contributing to the quiet trading day' (Associated Press). *Plus* is a preposition, not a conjunction, and therefore does not influence the number of the verb. Two and two are four, but two plus two is four. The example above should say 'was cited as a factor' or *plus* should be changed to 'and'.

podium. See LECTERN, PODIUM, DAIS, ROSTRUM.

populace, populous. The first describes a general population. The second means heavily populated.

populous. See POPULACE, POPULOUS.

pore, pour. Occasionally *pour* appears where *pore* is intended. As a verb, *pore* means to examine carefully ('He pored over the documents') or, more rarely, to meditate. *Pour* indicates a flow, either literally ('He poured the water down the drain') or figuratively ('The rioters poured through the streets').

poser, poseur. The first is a puzzle. The second is a person of affected manner.

poseur. See POSER, POSEUR.

position. Often a pointer to verbosity. 'They now find themselves in a position where they have to make a choice' (*Daily Telegraph*) would be immeasurably better as 'They now have to make a choice'.

possessives. Problems with possessives are discussed in some detail in the Appendix under APOSTROPHE, but three especially common faults are worth mentioning here.

1. Failure to put an apostrophe in the right place. This is particularly frequent with words like *men's*, *women's* and *children's*, which all too often appear as *mens'*, *womens'* and *childrens'*.

2. Failure to put in an apostrophe at all. This practice – spelling the words *mens*, *womens* and *childrens* and so on – is particularly rife among advertisers and retailers. It is painful enough to behold there, inexcusable elsewhere.

3. Putting an apostrophe where none is needed. Possessive pronouns – *his*, *hers*, *ours*, *theirs* and so on – do not take an apostrophe. But sometimes one is wrongly inserted, as here: 'I don't think much of your's' (*Independent* headline). (See also 'OURS IS NOT TO REASON WHY . . .').

(See also CHILDREN'S; MEN'S, WOMEN'S.)

possible is wrongly followed by 'may' in constructions such as the following: 'It is possible that she may decide to go after all' (*Daily Telegraph*). Make it either 'It is possible that she will decide to go after all' or 'She may decide to go after all'. Together the two words are unnecessary.

postmeridian, post meridiem. The first means related to or happening in the afternoon. The second, also pertaining to the period after noon, is the Latin term better known to most of us as the abbreviation p.m. Note the different terminal spellings.

post meridiem. See POSTMERIDIAN, POST MERIDIEM.

pour

pour. See PORE, POUR.

practicable. See PRACTICAL, PRACTICABLE.

practical, practicable. Anything that can be done *and* is worth doing is practical. Anything that can be done, whether or not it is worth doing, is practicable.

practice, practise. 'U.S. usage ... spells both noun and verb *practise*, as with *license*' (Fieldhouse, *Everyman's Good English Guide*). That is a common misconception outside North America. In the United States, *practice* is in fact always spelled with a 'c': *practice, practiced, practicing*. In British usage, the noun is spelled *practice* ('Practice makes perfect') and the verb *practise* ('You must practise your piano lessons').

practise. See PRACTICE, PRACTISE.

precautionary measure is a common phrase, but can nearly always be shortened simply to *precaution*.

precipitant, precipitate, precipitous. All three come from the same root, the Latin *praecipitare* ('to throw headlong'). *Precipitous* means very steep: cliff faces are precipitous. *Precipitant* and *precipitate* both indicate a headlong rush and are almost indistinguishable in meaning, but *precipitant* tends to emphasize the abruptness of the rush and *precipitate* the rashness of it. The most common error is to use *precipitous* to describe actions ('his precipitous departure from the Cabinet'). *Precipitous* can describe only physical characteristics.

precipitate. See PRECIPITANT, PRECIPITATE, PRECIPITOUS.

precipitous. See PRECIPITANT, PRECIPITATE, PRECIPITOUS.

precondition, preplanning, prerecorded, etc. Almost always redundant: 'A lot of headaches can be avoided with a little careful preplanning' (*Chicago Tribune*). All planning must be done in advance. *Pre-* adds nothing to its meaning and should be deleted, as it should have been in these examples: 'There are, however, three preconditions to be met before negotiations can begin' (*Guardian*); 'The company's music performance reflected both the volatility and opportunities for growth in the worldwide market for prerecorded music' (advertisement in the *Economist*).

premier, première. The first is a government official of top rank, especially a prime minister. The second is a début.

première. See PREMIER, PREMIÈRE.

premises is always plural when referring to property. There is no such thing as a business premise.

preplanning. See PRECONDITION, PREPLANNING, PRE-RECORDED, ETC.

prepositions. Anyone who believes that it is wrong to end a sentence with a preposition – and there are still some who do – is about a century out of touch. The 'rule' was enshrined by one Robert Lowth, an eighteenth-century Bishop of London and gentleman grammarian. In his wildly idiosyncratic but curiously influential *Short Introduction to English Grammar*, Lowth urged his readers not to end sentences with prepositions if they could decently avoid it. Too many people took him much too literally and for a century and a half the notion held sway. Today, happily, it is universally condemned as a pointless affectation. Indeed, there are many sentences where the preposition could scarcely come anywhere but at the end: 'This bed hasn't been slept in'; 'What is the world coming to?', 'I don't know what you are talking about'.

On a separate matter, a common fault among hurried or disorganized writers is to let prepositions pile up one after the other, as if the sentence were on some kind of automatic pilot. Consider this exceptional offering from *The Times* and note the abundance of *ofs* and *afters*: 'Bettaney . . . became the first member of the Security Service ever to be convicted of spying at the end of a trial held in camera after the first 35 minutes of the prosecution's opening to the return of the jury after a five-hour deliberation yesterday'. The sentence is effectively indecipherable.

prerecorded. See PRECONDITION, PREPLANNING, PRE-RECORDED, ETC.

prescribe, proscribe. *Prescribe* means to set down as a rule or guide. *Proscribe* means to denounce or prohibit. If you get bronchitis, your doctor may prescribe antibiotics and proscribe smoking.

present, presently. Like 'current' and 'currently', these two often appear needlessly in sentences, as here: 'A new factory, which is presently under construction in Manchester, will add to capacity' (*The Times*). The sentence says as much without *presently* as with it.

presently. See PRESENT, PRESENTLY.

pressurize. 'Esso accused him of trying to pressurize the Prime Minister into bailing out his petrochemical plant . . .' (*The Times*). Gases, liquids and foods can be pressurized (i.e., compacted into containers under pressure). People are pressed or pressured.

prestigious. A few die-hard authorities continue to insist that *prestigious* should be used only to describe that which is illusory or deceptive on the grounds that the word comes from the Latin *praestigiae*, meaning 'juggler's tricks'. That meaning has in fact been fading away since the early nineteenth century.

To defend the stricter meaning now on grounds of etymology is rather like insisting that 'silly' must, because of its derivation, mean happy and holy or that a villain is someone who works in a villa. Meanings change. When those changes appear to be for the worse, we might fairly try to get in their way. But with *prestigious* that would be neither practical nor desirable. People have been broadening its sense for almost 200 years, not as an act of defiance against the grammarians, but simply because the newer meaning was felt to be needed and the older was not. Today the original sense of the word is effectively dead everywhere but in the hearts of a scattering of purists. Most dictionaries now give the broader sense of 'worthy of esteem' as the only one, including (since 1976) one of the word's last defenders, *The Concise Oxford*.

presume. See ASSUME, PRESUME.

presumptive, presumptuous. The first is sometimes used when the second is intended. *Presumptuous* means impudent and inclined to take liberties, or to act in a manner that is excessively bold and forthright. *Presumptive* means giving grounds to presume and is primarily a technical term. The wrong use is seen here: 'She considered the question with the equanimity of someone who has long been immune to presumptive prying' (*Sunday Telegraph*).

presumptuous. See PRESUMPTIVE, PRESUMPTUOUS.

pretension but *pretentious*.

prevaricate, procrastinate. Occasionally confused. *Prevaricate* means to speak or act evasively, to stray from the truth. *Procrastinate* means to put off doing.

prevent often appears incorrectly in sentences such as this: 'They tried to prevent him leaving'. It should be: 'They tried to prevent his leaving' or 'They tried to prevent him from leaving'. (See GERUNDS (2).)

preventative. See PREVENTIVE, PREVENTATIVE.

preventive, preventative. 'One way to ease their difficulties, they decided, was to practise preventative medicine' (*Economist*). *Preventative* is not incorrect, but *preventive* is shorter.

prima facie. See A PRIORI, PRIMA FACIE.

principal, principle. *Principle* means fundamental and is usually applied to fundamental beliefs or truths ('It's not the money, it's the principle') or to fundamental understandings ('They have signed an agreement in principle'). It is always a noun. *Principal* can be a noun meaning chief or of first importance ('He is the school's principal') or an adjective with the same meaning ('The principal reason for my going . . .').

principle. See PRINCIPAL, PRINCIPLE.

prior to. See BEFORE, PRIOR TO.

pristine. '. . . the campaign waged by the anti-repeal forces was pristine clean' (cited by Kingsley Amis in *The State of the Language*). *Pristine* does not mean spotless, as was intended in the example above, or brand new, as is frequently intended elsewhere. It means original or primeval or in a state virtually unchanged from the original.

procrastinate. See PREVARICATE, PROCRASTINATE.

Procter & Gamble for the household products company. Often misspelled *Proctor*.

prodigal does not mean wandering or given to running away, a sense sometimes wrongly inferred from the parable of the Prodigal Son. It means recklessly wasteful or extravagant.

prognosis. See DIAGNOSIS, PROGNOSIS.

prohibit. See FORBID, PROHIBIT.

prone, prostrate, recumbent, supine. *Supine* means lying face upwards (it may help to remember that a supine person is on his spine). *Prone* and *prostrate* are regarded by most dictionaries and usage authorities – but by no means all – as meaning lying face downwards. (A few say that they can also apply to a person or thing lying face up.) *Prostrate* should, in any case, suggest throwing oneself down, either in submission or for protection; someone who is merely asleep should not be called prostrate. *Recumbent* means lying flat in any position, but, like repose, it should indicate a position of ease and comfort. For the other sense of *prone*, see LIABLE, LIKELY, APT, PRONE.

proper nouns. Many writers stumble when confronted with finding a plural form for a proper noun, as in the two following examples, both from *The Times* and both wrong: 'This is the first of a new series about the Rush's'; 'The Cox's were said by neighbours to be . . . happily married'. The rule for making plurals of proper nouns is precisely the same as for any other nouns. If you have no trouble turning 'one fox' into 'two foxes' or 'one church' into 'two churches', you should have no trouble making 'the Rush family' into 'the Rushes' and 'the Cox couple' into 'the Coxes'. In short, for names ending in 's', 'sh', 'ch' or 'x', add 'es'. Lewises, Lennoxes, Clemenses. For all others, simply add 's': Smiths, Browns, Greens, the two Koreas. The rule is invariable for Anglo-Saxon names. For others, there are a few exceptions, among them Rockies, Ptolemies, Alleghenies, Mercuries and (in some publications) Germanies. At all events, the addition of an apostrophe to make any noun plural is always wrong.

prophecy, prophesy. The first is the noun, the second the verb. Thus: 'I prophesy war; that is my prophecy'.

prophesy. See PROPHECY, PROPHESY.

proportion. See PERCENTAGE, PROPORTION.

proscribe. See PRESCRIBE, PROSCRIBE.

prostrate. See PRONE, PROSTRATE, RECUMBENT, SUPINE.

protagonist. Literally the word means 'first actor' (from the Greek *protos* and *agonistes*) and by extension may be applied to the person who most drives the action in any affair. However, there cannot properly be more than one protagonist per affair, as was evidently thought here: 'During the anomalous decade of the 1930s the three protagonists of this book each played out important . . . roles' (*The New York Times*). The word is not the opposite of *antagonist*, of which there can be any number. Nor does it necessarily have anything to do with heroic or admirable behaviour or bear any relationship to the Latin *pro-*, meaning 'for' or 'on behalf of'. A protagonist may champion a cause, and in practice often does, but that isn't implicit in the word.

prototype is the word for an original that serves as a model for later products of its type. Thus the qualifying descriptions in first prototype, experimental prototype and model prototype are generally redundant.

proved, proven. In general in British usage, *proved* is the preferred past tense form ('the accused was proved innocent') and *proven* the preferred form for adjectival uses ('a proven formula'). An exception is the Scottish legal term *not proven*, which is a formal finding and should be observed in newspaper reports and other formal writing.

proven. See PROVED, PROVEN.

proverbial. 'He stuck up the proverbial two fingers' (*Daily Mail*). Unless there is some connection to an actual proverb, the word is wrongly used and better avoided.

provided, providing. Most authorities consider the first preferable to the second in constructions such as 'He agreed to come provided he could get the day off work', but either would be correct. 'If' is often better still.

providing. See PROVIDED, PROVIDING.

purposefully. See PURPOSELY, PURPOSEFULLY.

purposely, purposefully. The first means intentionally. The second means with an objective in mind. 'She purposely nudged me' means it was no accident. 'She purposefully nudged me' means she did it to make a point or draw my attention to something.

put an end to is an expression to which one might usefully do just that. Make it 'stop'.

pyrrhic victory is not, as is sometimes thought, a hollow triumph. It is one won at a huge cost to the victor.

Q

Qantas. Although the full name is no longer used, for historical purposes it is worth noting that Qantas is short for Queensland and Northern Territory Aerial Service. Not *Air* and not *Services*.

quadriplegia, not *quadra-*, for paralysis of all four limbs.

quadruped, not *quadri-* or *quadra-*, for a four-legged animal.

quandary. Not *quandry* or *quandery*.

quantum leap has become a cliché and is better avoided. A separate objection is that its general sense of a dramatic step forward is at variance with its actual scientific sense of a movement or advance that is discrete and measurable, but not necessarily, or even usually, dramatic.

Queen's College, Oxford, but *Queens' College*, Cambridge.

query, inquiry, enquiry. A query is a single question. An inquiry or enquiry may be a single question or an extensive investigation. Either spelling is correct, but *inquiry* is preferred by most dictionaries in both Britain and America.

question, leading. A leading question is not a challenging or hostile one, as is sometimes thought, but the opposite. It is a question designed to encourage the person being questioned to make the desired response. A lawyer who says to a witness, 'You didn't see the murder, did you?' has asked a leading question.

question mark has become an overworked embellishment of the expression 'a question hanging over', which is itself wearyingly overused. Consider: 'The case . . . has raised a question mark over the competence of British security' (*The Times*). Would you say of a happy event that it had raised an exclamation mark over the proceedings or that a pause in negotiations had a comma hanging over them?

quinquennial can mean either to last for five years or to occur every five years. Because of the inherent ambiguity the word is almost always better replaced with a more specific phrase.

quite. Because *quite* means positively or completely, some authorities object to its use where it creates an air of redundancy, as in 'quite all right or 'quite similar'. Such expressions are sometimes a little quaint and often better avoided in formal writing, but equally they could be defended as idiomatic.

quoting in fragments is often a needless distraction, as here: 'He said that profits in the second half would be "good"' (*The Times*). Quoted matter, especially when in fragments, should have some justification. When the word or words being quoted are unusual or unexpected or particularly descriptive ('It was, he said, a "lousy" performance') or are otherwise notable, the use of inverted commas is always unobjectionable and often advisable. But to set off a workaday word like 'good' in the example above is unnecessary. Here is a sentence in which the second set of quotation marks is as unobjectionable as the first is fatuous: 'Dietz agreed that loneliness was a "feature" of Hinckley's life but he added that studies have shown that "loneliness is as common as the common cold in winter"' (*Washington Post*).

A separate, grammatical danger of quoting in fragments is seen here: 'Although he refused to be drawn on the future of the factory, Sir Kenneth said that the hope of finding a buyer "was not out of the question"' (*The Times*). Clearly Sir Kenneth would have said, 'That is not out of the question', not 'That was not out of the question'. In quoted material, even when fragmentary, the tense must be preserved.

A final problem is the tendency of some writers to put the words of one person into the mouths of many, as here: 'Witnesses at the scene said that there was "a tremendous bang and then all hell broke loose"' (*Guardian*). The comment should be paraphrased or attributed to just one witness.

R

rack, wrack. 'It noted that its reserves constituted a very slender margin of safety in a world increasingly wracked by political risks' (*The Times*). *Wrack* is an archaic variant of *wreck* and now almost never appears except in the expression 'wrack and ruin'. *Rack*, the word intended in the quotation, means to put under strain. The expressions are 'nerve-racking' and 'to rack one's brains'.

Radio Telefís Éireann for the Irish broadcasting corporation.

radius. The plural can be either *radii* or *radiuses*.

raining cats and dogs. No one knows what inspired this expression, but it is worth noting that in 1738, when Swift condemned it, it was already hackneyed.

ranges of figures. 'Profits in the division were expected to rise by between $35 and $45 million' (*Observer*). Although most people will see at once that the writer meant to indicate a range of $10 million, literally she was saying that profits could be as little as $35 or as much as $45 million. If you mean 'between $35 million and $45 million' it is generally better to say so.

Ranks Hovis McDougall for the British food group. Not *Rank*.

rapt, wrapped. One is rapt in thought, not wrapped. *Rapt* means engrossed, absorbed, enraptured.

rarefaction. See RAREFY, RAREFACTION.

rarefy, rarefaction. Not *rari-*.

ravage, ravish. The first means to lay waste. The second means to rape or carry off – or, a touch confusingly, to enrapture. Clearly in all senses, for both words, care needs to be exercised to avoid confusion.

ravish. See RAVAGE, RAVISH.

raze. 'Zurich's Autonomous Youth Centre was razed to the ground yesterday' (*The Times*). The ground is the only place to which a structure can be razed. It is enough to say: 'Zurich's Autonomous Youth Centre was razed yesterday'.

razzamatazz. See RAZZMATAZZ, RAZZAMATAZZ.

razzmatazz, razzamatazz. The first is generally the preferred spelling, but most dictionaries also accept the second. A common misspelling is seen here: 'For them the promotional razamataz is much more about holding on to what they have' (*The Times*).

react is better reserved for spontaneous responses ('He reacted to the news by fainting'). It should not be used to indicate responses marked by reflection, as it was here: 'The Vice-President's lawyers were not expected to react to the court's decision before Monday at the earliest' (*Los Angeles Times*).

reason ... is because is a common construction, and has been for at least 200 years, but it continues to be criticized as a tautology by many authorities. Consider an example from the *Observer*: 'The reason she spends less and less time in England these days is because her business interests keep her constantly on the move'. Those authorities who object to such constructions (and not all do) maintain that the sentence would be better with *because* deleted or replaced with 'that'. They are right about the tautology but, I would submit, wrong (or at least somewhat off beam) about the remedy. The fault in such sentences lies at the front end. Remove 'the reason' (and its attendant verb 'is') and in most cases a crisper, more focused sentence emerges: 'She spends less and less time in England these days because her business interests keep her constantly on the move'.

reason why, like *reason . . . is because* (see above), is generally redundant. Consider these two examples: 'If they don't, great bands of shareholders will want to know the reason why' (*Daily Mail*); 'His book argues that the main reason why inner-city blacks are in such a sorry state is not because whites are prejudiced but because low-skilled jobs near their homes are disappearing' (*Economist*). An improvement can nearly always be effected by removing one word or the other – e.g., 'the reason' from the first example, 'why' from the second.

reckless. Not *wreckless*, unless you are describing a setting in which there are no wrecks.

reconstruction. 'The play is a dramatic reconstruction of what might happen when a combination of freak weather conditions threatens to flood London' (*The Times*). As a moment's reflection should have made apparent to the writer, you cannot reconstruct an event that has not yet happened. *Re-* is often prefixed to words where it adds no meaning, for instance *reduplicate* and *recopy*.

recumbent. See PRONE, PROSTRATE, RECUMBENT, SUPINE.

reduce. See DEPLETE, REDUCE.

redundant. See TAUTOLOGY, REDUNDANCY, PLEONASM, SOLECISM.

refute means to show conclusively that an allegation is wrong. It does not mean simply to dispute or deny a contention.

regretfully, regrettably. The first means with feelings of regret: 'Regretfully they said their farewells'. The second means unfortunately: 'Regrettably I did not have enough money to buy it'.

regrettably. See REGRETFULLY, REGRETTABLY.

reiterate. Since *iterate* means repeat, *reiterate* ought to mean re-repeat, but it doesn't. It also just means repeat. A common fault is seen here: 'She hopes her message to the markets, reiterated again at the weekend, will be enough to prevent the pound sliding further' (*The Times*). 'Again' is always superfluous with *re-* words (reiterate, repeat, reaffirm) and should be deleted.

relatively, like *comparatively*, should not be used unless there is some sense of a comparison or relationship. As often as not, the word can be removed without loss, as here: 'The group has taken the relatively bold decision to expand its interests in Nigeria' (*The Times*). (See also COMPARATIVELY.)

relevant. See GERMANE, RELEVANT, MATERIAL.

relieve. See ALLAY, ALLEVIATE, ASSUAGE, RELIEVE.

remunerate. 'Metathesis' is the term for transposing sounds or letters, which is what often happens with this word, as here: 'Mr Strage said in the witness box that he was to receive fair renumeration for his work' (*Independent*). The urge to associate *remunerate* with words of quantity like 'numeral' and 'enumerate' is understandable, but in fact the words spring from different sources. *Remunerate* comes from the Latin *munus* (by which it is related to *munificent*). 'Numeral', 'enumerate' and other related words come from the Latin *numerus*.

rendezvous is the spelling for both the singular and plural.

repel, repulse. Not to be confused. *Repulse* means to drive back: 'The army repulsed the enemy's attack'. It should not be confused with *repulsive*, meaning to cause repugnance. *Repel* is the word for causing squeamishness or distaste: 'The idea of eating squid repelled her'.

repetition. Many authorities are rightly critical of what Bernstein called 'synonymomania' – the almost pathological dread among some journalists of using the same word twice in one article. The practice is particularly rife among that odd strain of sportswriters who feel compelled, on second reference, to refer to boxers as pugilists and ringmasters, and baseballs as leather spheroids, and that sort of thing. It is almost always better to repeat a word than to resort to some feeble or contrived synonym.

However, one kind of repetition often is better avoided, and that is when connective words like *which, when, who, because* and *where* are repeated in the same sentence. Consider two examples: 'The takeover, which was originally agreed on amiable terms, was blocked by the Monopolies Commission, which is not expected to make a decision for some time' (*The Times*); 'A similar sequence of events was responsible for the Aberfan tragedy in 1966 when 116 children died when a sliding coal waste tip engulfed the village school and a row of houses' (*Independent*). Such sentences frequently, though not invariably, are awkward and confusing. Too many ideas are jostling for our attention at once. Generally, an improvement can be effected by breaking the sentences into two.

replica. Properly, a replica is an exact copy, built to the same scale as the original and using the same materials. To use the word when you might better use 'model', 'miniature', 'copy' or 'reproduction' devalues it, as here: 'Using nothing but plastic Lego toy bricks, they have painstakingly reconstructed replicas of some of the world's most famous landmarks' (*Sunday Times*).

repulse. See REPEL, REPULSE.

responsible. A few authorities continue to point out that responsibility for events can lie only with people and not with things. Poor maintenance might be responsible for a fire, but lightning could not be. It could cause a fire or ignite a fire, but it could not properly be said to be responsible for it.

restaurateur. I recently watched a cookery programme in which the presenter repeatedly referred to a proprietor of a restaurant as a 'restauranter'. The same error occasionally appears in leading newspapers. If you don't know it already, note now that there is no 'n' in *restaurateur*.

restive. Originally the word meant balky, refusing to move or budge, but through confusion has come to be used more and more as a synonym for restless. Most dictionaries now recognize both senses, but if the word is to have any special value it should contain at least some suggestion of resistance. A crowd of protesters may grow restive upon the arrival of mounted police, but a person sitting uncomfortably on a hard bench is better described as restless.

revenge. See AVENGE, REVENGE.

reverse. See CONTRARY, CONVERSE, OPPOSITE, REVERSE.

revert back is commonly seen and always redundant: 'If no other claimant can be found, the right to the money will revert back to her' (*Daily Telegraph*). Delete *back*.

re- words. In America, mystifyingly, many publications show a formidable resistance to putting hyphens into any word beginning with *re-*. Yet often the presence or absence of a hyphen can usefully and immediately denote a difference in meaning, as between *recollect* (remember) and *re-collect* (collect again), or between *recede* (withdraw) and *re-cede* (give back again, as with territory), or between *recreation* (leisure activity) and *re-creation* (the act of creating again). My advice, for what it is worth, is always to insert a hyphen if you think it might reduce the chance of even momentary misunderstanding.

Rime of the Ancient Mariner, The, not *Rhyme*, for the 1798 poem by Samuel Taylor Coleridge.

rostrum. See LECTERN, PODIUM, DAIS, ROSTRUM.

Rottweiler for the breed of dog. Note *-tt-*, one 'l'.

S

saccharin, saccharine. The first is an artificial sweetener; the second means sugary.

saccharine. See SACCHARIN, SACCHARINE.

sacrilegious. Sometimes misspelled *sacreligious* on the mistaken assumption that *religious* is part of the word. It isn't.

Sahara. 'His intention is to cross the Sahara Desert alone' (*San Francisco Chronicle*). It is perhaps pedantic to press the point too fiercely, but it is worth noting that Sahara means desert, so the common expression Sahara Desert is clearly redundant.

St Catherine's College. See CATHARINE'S, CATHERINE'S.

St Helens. See HELENS, ST.

St James's. See JAMES'S, ST.

St Katharine's Docks. See KATHARINE'S DOCKS, ST.

St Kitts-Nevis. See KITTS-NEVIS, ST.

salutary. Not *-tory*. For a discussion of its usage, see HEALTHY, HEALTHFUL, SALUTARY.

Salvadoran, not *-ean*, for a person or thing from El Salvador.

Sam Browne, not *Brown*, for the type of belt worn diagonally across the chest.

sandal for the type of shoe. Not *sandle*.

sanitary. Not *-tory*.

Sara Lee, not *Sarah*, for the US food company.

sarcasm. See IRONY, SARCASM.

Sauterne, Sauternes. The first is a sweet French wine; the second is the village in Gironde from which it comes.

Sauternes. See SAUTERNE, SAUTERNES.

savoir-faire, savoir-vivre. Both are French, of course. The first indicates social grace, the second good breeding.

savoir-vivre. See SAVOIR-FAIRE, SAVOIR-VIVRE.

Sca Fell and **Scafell Pike** are nearby but separate mountains in Cumbria. The latter is the highest eminence in England at 3,206 feet.

Scafell Pike. See SCA FELL and SCAFELL PIKE.

Scalextric, for the brand of miniature racing sets, is probably mispronounced more often than it is misspelled, but the unusual name is in either case worth noting.

Scarborough for the town in North Yorkshire, but *Earl of Scarbrough* for the peerage.

scarfs. See SCARVES, SCARFS.

scarves, scarfs. Either is correct for the plural of scarf.

scary. Not *-ey*.

Schiphol Airport, Amsterdam.

scrutiny. The word is a magnet for superfluous adjectives, as here: 'Mr Shultz's activities are expected to attract close scrutiny' (*The New York Times*). *Scrutiny* means to give careful attention, so close scrutiny, careful scrutiny and the like are redundant. Bernstein, who often cautioned against the solecism, actually commits it himself in *The Careful Writer* when he says: 'Under close scrutiny, many constructions containing the word "not" make no sense . . .'. In the same volume he unwittingly underlines the point by urging writers to 'scrutinize thoughtfully every phrase that eases itself almost mechanically onto the paper'. Had he followed his own advice, he no doubt would have omitted 'thoughtfully' there.

scurrilous, which is most often encountered in the expression 'a scurrilous attack', does not mean disreputable or specious, though those senses are often intended. It means grossly obscene or abusive. An attack must be exceedingly harsh to be scurrilous.

second largest and other similar comparisons often lead writers astray: 'Japan is the second largest drugs market in the world after the United States' (*The Times*). Not quite. It is the largest drugs market in the world after the United States or it is the second largest drugs market in the world. The sentence above could be fixed by placing a comma after 'world'.

Securities and Exchange Commission, not *Securities Exchange Commission*, for the body that regulates US stock markets.

seismogram. See SEISMOMETER, SEISMOGRAPH, SEIS-MOGRAM.

seismograph. See SEISMOMETER, SEISMOGRAPH, SEIS-MOGRAM.

seismometer, seismograph, seismogram. Sometimes confused. A *seismometer* is a sensor placed in the earth to record earthquakes and other vibrations. A *seismograph* is the instrument that records the seismometer's readings. A *seismogram* is the printout or chart that provides a visual record of seismic activity.

self-confessed, as in 'a self-confessed murderer', is usually tautological. In most cases, *confessed* alone is enough.

sensual, sensuous. The words are only broadly synonymous. *Sensual* applies to a person's baser instincts as distinguished from reason. It should always hold connotations of sexual allure or lust. *Sensuous* was coined by Milton to avoid those connotations and to suggest instead the idea of being alive to sensations. It should be used when no suggestion of sexual arousal is intended.

sensuous. See SENSUAL, SENSUOUS.

sentences, length of. Occasionally a proliferation of connecting words produces a sentence that simply runs away with itself. I offer the following as a classic of its type: 'But dramatic price shifts are not expected by the oil companies because retail prices are already claimed to be about 8p a gallon cheaper than is justified by the drop in crude oil price which anyway because taxation accounts for 70 per cent of the price of a retail gallon has a relatively limited impact' (*The Times*).

septuagenarian for a person in his or her seventies. Note the 'u', which often goes astray, as here: 'Even Chairman Mao created his own athletic image with his septagenarian plunge into the Yangtse' (*Sunday Times*).

Serengeti for the plain and famed national park in Tanzania. Not -*getti*.

servicing. See SERVING, SERVICING.

serving, servicing. 'Cable TV should be servicing half the country within five years' (*Daily Mail*). Bulls service cows. Mechanics service faulty machinery. But cable TV systems serve the country. *Servicing* is better reserved for the idea of installation and maintenance. *Serve* is the better word for describing things that are of general and continuing benefit.

sewage, sewerage. *Sewage* is waste; *sewerage* is the system that carries the waste away.

sewerage. See SEWAGE, SEWERAGE.

Shakespearean. See SHAKESPEARIAN, SHAKESPEAREAN.

Shakespearian, Shakespearean. The first is the usual spelling in Britain and the second is the usual spelling in America, but, interestingly, don't look to *The Oxford English Dictionary* for guidance on this one. Perversely and charmingly, but entirely unhelpfully, the *OED* insists on spelling the name Shakspere, a decision it based on one of the six spellings Shakespeare himself used. It does, however, acknowledge that Shakespeare is 'perhaps' the commonest spelling now used.

shall, will. Authorities have been trying to pin down the vagaries and nuances of *shall* and *will* since the seventeenth century. In *The King's English*, the Fowler brothers devote twenty pages to discussing the matter. The gist of what they have to say is that either you understand the distinctions instinctively or you do not; that if you don't, you probably never will; and that if you do, you don't need to be told anyway.

The rule most frequently propounded is that to express simple futurity you should use *shall* in the first person and *will* in the second and third persons, and to express determination (or volition) you should do the reverse. But by that rule Churchill blundered grammatically when he vowed: 'We shall fight in the fields and in the streets, we shall fight in the hills; we shall never surrender'. As did MacArthur when he said at Corregidor: 'I shall return'. As have all those who have ever sung 'We Shall Overcome'.

The simple fact is that whether you use *shall* or *will* in a given instance depends very much on your age and your birthplace and the emphasis with which you mean to express yourself. The English tend to use *shall* more frequently and more specifically than do the Scots or Irish or Americans, but even in England the distinctions are rapidly fading and by no means fixed.

In short, it is not possible to make binding rules to distinguish between the two and (dare I say it?) no longer all that important anyway.

Shalott, The Lady of, for the 1832 poem by Alfred, Lord Tennyson. Not *Shallot*.

shambles. Used in the sense of a mess or muddle, the word was long objected to by purists, notably Fowler, who cited this as a slipshod usage: 'The Colonial Secretary denied ... that the conference on the future of Malta had been a shambles'. *Shambles* originally meant a slaughterhouse, and by extension it came to be used to describe any scene of carnage or bloodshed. That remains its primary meaning, but the looser sense of mere disorderliness is now well established. Both *The Concise Oxford* and *American Heritage* give that meaning without comment.

Shangri-La, not *-la*, for the paradise created by James Hilton in the 1933 novel *Lost Horizon*.

Shepherd Market, but *Shepherd's Bush*, both London.

Shetland or **the Shetland Islands** are the accepted designations for the Scottish islands. *The Shetlands* is frowned on by some and thus better avoided. See also ORKNEY.

should like. 'I should have liked to have seen it' is a common construction and may be excused in conversation, but in writing it should be 'I should like to have seen it' or 'I should have liked to see it'. For American usage, read 'would' for 'should'.

Sidney Sussex College, Cambridge. Not *Sydney.*

'Sign of Four, The', not *the Four,* for the Sherlock Holmes story.

simile. See METAPHOR, SIMILE.

since. 'She gave strong support to the visions of the late Bernard Kilgore and the other executives and editors who operated the Journal and Dow Jones since World War II' (*Wall Street Journal*); 'Since April the Inland Revenue stopped giving immediate tax refunds to those who were unlucky enough to become unemployed' (*The Times*). *Since* indicates action starting at a specified time in the past and continuing up to the present. The verbs in sentences in which it appears must also indicate action that is still continuing – that is, they should be 'have operated' in the first instance and 'has stopped' in the second.

Sisyphus. Not *-ss-*. In Greek mythology, Sisyphus was a king of Corinth who was condemned for eternity to push a heavy stone up a hill, only to have it roll down again. Hence *Sisyphean* describes some endless task.

situation is almost always needlessly deployed in constructions such as this: 'The exchange ... had failed to be alert to the potential of a crisis situation as it developed' (*The New York Times*). Usually, as here, the word can be deleted without loss.

skulduggery. Often misspelled *skull-*, as here: 'Political skullduggeries are as much at home in Louisiana as crawfish and beignets' (*Time* magazine). So far as is known, the word has nothing to do with the bony part of the head; it is a modified form of *sculdudderie*, a word of uncertain provenance, which originally signified sexual misbehaviour.

slander. See LIBEL, SLANDER.

sleight of hand. Not *slight*. *Sleight*, meaning dexterity or deceptiveness, comes from the Old Norse *sloegdh*, and *slight*, meaning slender or frail, comes from the Old Norse *slettr*, but they have nothing else in common except their pronunciations.

Soane's Museum, Sir John, London. Note the apostrophe.

so as to. The first two words can generally be deleted without loss, as they might have been here: '. . . the rest of the crowd stuffed hot dogs into their faces so as to avoid being drawn into the discussion' (*The New York Times*).

solecism. See TAUTOLOGY, REDUNDANCY, PLEONASM, SOLECISM.

some. Many journalists of a certain age appear to have had it drilled into them that *some* in the sense of an unknown or unquantified number is a casualism to be avoided at all costs, as in 'There were some 40 passengers on the ship'. The belief is without any real basis. The sense of approximately or about has long been well established. However, there is at least one good reason for regarding the word with some suspicion. Consider this passage from a *New York Times* article: 'Since 1981, according to Hewitt's survey of some 530 companies, some 24,000 employees quit jobs under such plans. Last year alone, some 74 plans were in effect'. Particularly when used repeatedly, as in the example just cited, the word lends writing a timid and equivocal ring, leaving the impression that the reporter lacked the resolve or initiative to find out just how many companies, plans and employees actually were involved. 'Some 40 passengers' and the like are defensible when the reference is incidental or in passing, but when the figures are integral to a discussion, *some* can look decidedly slapdash and is generally better replaced by more positive expressions: 'more than 500 companies', 'an estimated 24,000 employees', 'at least 70 plans'. In any case, it is worth noting that the middle *some* in the example above ('some 24,000 employees') could be deleted without the slightest danger of being over-rash. Large, round numbers are almost always construed as being approximate. You do not need to qualify them.

sometime, some time. Most often it is one word: 'They will arrive sometime tomorrow'. But when *some* is used as an adjective equivalent to 'a short' or 'a long' or 'an indefinite', it should be two words: 'The announcement was made some time ago'.

Three considerations may help you to make the distinction:

1. *Some time* as two words is usually preceded by a preposition ('for some time', 'at some time') or followed by a helping word ('some time ago').

2. *Some time* can always be replaced with an equivalent expression ('a short time ago', 'a long time ago', etc.); *sometime* cannot.

3. When spoken, greater stress is placed on time when *some time* is two words.

some time. See SOMETIME, SOME TIME.

sort. 'Mr Hawkins said that Mr Webster was a pretty seasoned operator when it came to dealing with these sort of things' (*The Times*). Make it 'this sort of thing' or 'these sorts of things'.

spate. 'The recent spate of takeover offers had focused attention on the sector' (*Observer*). The reference here was to half a dozen takeover offers – a flurry. *Spate* should be used to describe a torrent. (See also PLETHORA.)

special, especial. The first means for a particular purpose, the second to a high degree. A special meal may be especially delicious.

species. See GENUS, SPECIES.

spit. See EXPECTORATE, SPIT.

split compound verbs. Some writers, apparently inspired by a misguided dread of the split infinitive (which see), are equally fastidious about not breaking up compound verbs, whatever the cost to idiom and clarity. (A compound verb is one made up of two elements, such as *has been, will go, is doing*.) The practice is particularly rife in America, where sentences like the following are often encountered: 'It is yet to be demonstrated that a national magazine effectively can cover cable listings' (*Wall Street Journal*); 'Hitler never has been portrayed with more credibility' (*Boston Globe*); 'It always has stood as one of the last great events in amateur sports' (*Los Angeles Times*).

It cannot be stressed vigorously enough that there is no harm in placing an adverb between the two elements of a compound verb. It contravenes no rule and flouts no authority. It is usually the natural place – and frequently the only place – for an adverb to go.

Those writers who so scrupulously avoid offending the integrity of a compound verb must be unaware that they disregard their self-imposed restriction every time they write 'He is not going' or 'Is it raining?' Otherwise they would have to change those sentences to 'He is going not' and 'Is raining it?' That would hardly be more illogical and contorted than 'effectively can cover' and 'always has stood'.

There are, of course, many instances in which the adverb can happily stand apart from the compound verb – 'He was working feverishly'; 'You must go directly to bed'; 'The time is passing quickly' – but forcibly evicting it for the sake of making words conform to some arbitrary pattern does no service to any passage.

split infinitives. It is almost certainly safe to say that the number of people who would never split an infinitive is a good deal larger than the number of people who actually know what an infinitive is and does.

That may account for the number of misconceptions that litter the issue. One is the belief that the split infinitive is a grammatical error. It is not. If it is an error at all, it is a rhetorical fault – a question of style – and not a grammatical one. Another is the curiously persistent belief that the split infinitive is widely condemned. That too is untrue. Almost no authority flatly condemns it. No one would argue that a split infinitive is a thing of beauty, but it is certainly no worse than some of the excruciating constructions foisted on readers by those who regard it with an almost pathological dread. Consider these three sentences, all from *The Times* and all with a certain ring of desperation about them: 'The agreement is unlikely significantly to increase the average price'; 'It was a nasty snub for the Stock Exchange and caused it radically to rethink its ideas'; 'The education system had failed adequately to meet the needs of industry and commerce, he said'.

The problem of the split infinitive arises because of a conflict between the needs of the infinitive and the needs of an adverb. The natural position for the two elements of a full infinitive is together: 'He proceeded to climb the ladder'. With adverbs the most natural position is, very generally, just before the verb: 'He slowly climbed the ladder'. The conflict comes when the two are brought together: 'He proceeded to slowly climb the ladder'.

The authorities are almost unanimously agreed that there is no reason to put the needs of the infinitive above the needs of the adverb. In practice the problem can usually be sidestepped. Most adverbs are portable and can be moved to a position from which they can perform their function without interfering with the infinitive. In the example above, for instance, we could say: 'He proceeded to climb the ladder slowly' or 'Slowly he proceeded to climb the ladder'. But that is not to say that there is any grammatical basis for regarding the infinitive as inviolable.

When moving the adverb produces ambiguity, the cure is at

least as bad as the disease. Consider again one of those *Times* sentences: 'The education system had failed adequately to meet the needs of industry and commerce . . .'. Literally the sentence is telling us that the education system had set out to fail and had done so adequately. Sometimes, indeed, it is all but impossible not to split the infinitive and preserve any sense. Bernstein cites these constructions, all crying out to be left alone: 'to more than double', 'to at least maintain', 'to all but ensure'.

If you wish, you may remain blindly intolerant of the split infinitive, but you should do so with the understanding that you are without the support of a single authority of standing. Even Partridge, normally the most conservative of arbiters, is against you. He says: 'Avoid the split infinitive wherever possible; but if it is the clearest and most natural construction, use it boldly. The angels are on our side'.

spoonfuls, not *spoonsful* or *spoons full*. Bernstein cites the following: 'Now throw in two tablespoons full of chopped parsley and cook ten minutes more. The quail ought to be tender by then'. As Bernstein drily adds, 'Never mind the quail; how are we ever going to get those tablespoons tender?'

stalactite, stalagmite. *Stalactites* point downwards, *stalagmites* upwards.

stalagmite. See STALACTITE, STALAGMITE.

stalemate. 'Senators Back Rise in Proposed Oil Tax as Stalemate Ends' (*New York Times* headline). Stalemates don't end. A chess match that reaches stalemate is not awaiting a more decisive outcome; the stalemate is the outcome. 'Standoff', the word the writer probably had in mind, or 'deadlock' would have been much better choices here.

Stamford, Stanford. Occasionally confused. Stamford is the name of notable communities in Lincolnshire and Connecticut.

Stanford is the university in Palo Alto, California. The intelligence test is the Stanford-Binet test.

stanch, staunch. 'He showed how common soldiers ... had fought their fears, staunched their wounds and met their deaths' (*Newsweek*). Although *staunch* is given as an acceptable variant by most dictionaries, *stanch* is still generally the preferred spelling for the verb. As an adjective, *staunch* is the only spelling ('a staunch supporter').

Stanford. See STAMFORD, STANFORD.

stationary, stationery. The difference in spelling goes back centuries, though etymologically there isn't any basis for it. Both words come from the Latin *stationarius* and both originally meant 'standing in a fixed position'. Stationers were tradesmen, usually booksellers, who sold their wares from a fixed spot (as opposed to itinerants). Today in Britain stationery is still sold by stationers, which makes the misspelling here less excusable, if no less frequent. It applies, incidentally, not just to writing paper and envelopes but to all office materials. Strictly speaking, paper clips and pencils are stationery.

stationery. See STATIONARY, STATIONERY.

staunch. See STANCH, STAUNCH.

straitjacket is often misspelled, as here: 'She was beaten, put into a home-made straightjacket and fed mustard sandwiches' (*Standard*). *Strait* means confined and restricted, as in 'straitened circumstances' or (in a more metaphorical sense) 'strait-laced'. Apart from the pronunciation, it has nothing in common with 'straight'.

strata, stratum. The first is sometimes used when the second is intended, as it was here: 'They dug into another strata and at last found what they were looking for' (*Daily Express*). A single level is a *stratum*. *Strata* signifies more than one.

Stratford-on-Avon, Stratford-upon-Avon. Most gazetteers and other reference sources give Stratford-upon-Avon as the correct name for the Warwickshire town. Some, like *The Oxford Dictionary for Writers and Editors*, are quite insistent about it. But it is worth noting that the local authority calls itself Stratford-on-Avon District Council. Thus, to be strictly accurate, you would have to accord the town one preposition and the council another.

Stratford-upon-Avon. See STRATFORD-ON-AVON, STRATFORD-UPON-AVON.

stratum. See STRATA, STRATUM.

strike action is in danger of becoming the invariable form in Britain, as in sentences such as this: 'The report says 2,500 engineers and technicians are threatening strike action because of the crisis' (*Sunday Times*). Why not 'are threatening to strike'?

stupefaction. See STUPEFIED, STUPEFACTION.

stupefied, stupefaction. All too often misspelled, as here: 'The owners sit inside, stupified in the sun, or venture out on to camp stools . . .' (*Sunday Times*); 'The 57-year-old evangelist denies four charges of rape and three of administering a stupifying drug' (*Independent*). Don't confuse the spelling with *stupid*. A similar erroneous exchange of 'i' for 'e' often happens with 'liquefy' and 'liquefaction' and 'rarefy' and 'rarefaction'.

stupor. Not -*our*.

subjunctives. The subjunctive, one of the four moods of verbs, has been slipping from use in English for decades. It is the mood seen in sentences like 'Although he die now, his name will live for ever'. Although once very common, it scarcely features in English now except in three types of construction. These are:

1. In certain stock phrases: 'be that as it may', 'far be it from me', 'so be it', 'as it were', 'God forbid' and many others. These are well established as idioms and normally cause no trouble.

2. In expressions involving suppositions or hypotheses: 'If I were you, I wouldn't go'; 'If she were in my position, she'd do the same thing', etc. These are the most problematic form of the subjunctive for most users and are discussed at some length under WILL, WOULD and IF.

3. Following verbs of command or request. Interestingly, this problem scarcely exists in America, where this form of the subjunctive has always been part of the native speech, but it is endlessly encountered in Britain at all levels of writing. In the following examples, the correct form is given in brackets: 'The Senate has now rewritten the contract insisting that the Navy considers [consider] other options' (*Daily Mail*); 'Opec's monitoring committee has recommended that the cartel's output ceiling remains [remain] unchanged'; 'No wonder the Tory Party turned him down as a possible candidate, suggesting he went away [go away] and came back [come back] with a better public image' (*Guardian*). In each instance it might help to imagine placing a 'should' just before the problem verb (e.g., 'suggesting he should go away'). Gowers in fact suggests that such sentences would be better in British usage if 'should' were inserted in every instance. It certainly wouldn't hurt.

substitute can be followed only by 'for'. You substitute one thing for another. If you find yourself following the word with 'by' or with any other preposition, you should choose another verb.

subsume. As Safire notes, the word has a great appeal to those who cannot resist a pretentious variation, but it is also frequently misused. It does not mean to consume or make subordinate, as is often thought. It means to be considered as part of a greater whole. *The Shorter OED* gives this example: 'In the judgment "all horses are animals", the conception "horses" is subsumed under that of "animals"'. In short, it is not a word that most writers in most contexts will often need.

successfully. 'Japanese researchers have successfully developed a semiconductor chip made of gallium arsenide' (Associated Press). It was thoughtful of the writer to tell us that the researchers had not unsuccessfully developed a gallium arsenide chip, but also unnecessary. Delete *successfully*.

supersede is one of the most frequently misspelled of words. Those who habitually make it *supercede* may take some comfort in knowing that the word caused just as much trouble to the ancient Romans, who often could not decide between *supersedere* and *supercedere*. *Supercede* was in early English usage an acceptable variant, but no longer.

supine. See PRONE, PROSTRATE, RECUMBENT, SUPINE.

Surinam. See SURINAME, SURINAM.

Suriname, Surinam. Confusion still occasionally arises concerning the name of this small South American country. *The Encarta World English Dictionary*, for instance, calls it Suriname under its main entry, but labels it Surinam on a map elsewhere in the same volume. The spelling Surinam can now safely be regarded as historic and Suriname as the correct modern spelling. The Suriname River and Suriname toad also take the modern spellings.

surrounded. 'Often shrouded by fog and surrounded on three sides by surging seas, the gray stone lighthouse looms like a medieval keep' (*Time* magazine); 'The waterworks is right in the middle of suburban Sutton and completely surrounded by houses' (*Sunday Express*). The first usage is wrong, the second superfluous.

If you are not completely encircled, you are not surrounded. *Surrounded* should be changed in the first example to 'cut off' or 'bordered' and 'completely' should be deleted from the second.

sympathy. See EMPATHY, SYMPATHY.

T

take place. See OCCUR, TAKE PLACE.

Tales of Hoffmann, The, is the title of the 1881 opera by Jacques Offenbach. Note *-ff-* and *-nn-*.

Tallinn for the capital of Estonia.

Taoiseach, the Prime Minister of Ireland. Pronounced *tee'-sock*.

tarantella for the type of Neapolitan dance. Not to be confused, of course, with *tarantula*, the type of spider.

target. To most people there are just two things you can do with a target: you can hit it or you can miss it. But for journalists and politicians, targets are things to be achieved, attained, exceeded, expanded, reduced, obtained, met, beaten and overtaken. As a consequence, their statements, if taken literally, can become absurd, as here: 'More welcome news came with the announcement that the public sector borrowing requirement now appears likely to undershoot its target for the full year' (*The Times*). An archer who undershoots a target will be chagrined. A politician will apparently be pleased. The reader may merely be puzzled.

In practice, *target* often is the most efficient word for conveying a point, even if the literal meaning is sometimes strained, but it is worth seeing if 'objective' or 'plan' wouldn't work as well.

Even more worth watching are instances in which *target* gets mixed up with other metaphors. Philip Howard cites this curious headline from *The Times*: '£6m ceiling keeps rise in earnings well within Treasury target'.

tautology, redundancy, pleonasm, solecism. Although various authorities detect various shades of distinction between the first three words, those distinctions are always very slight and, on comparison, are frequently contradictory. Essentially all three mean using more words than necessary to convey an idea.

Not all repetition is bad. It may be used for effect, as in poetry, or for clarity, or in deference to idiom. 'Opec countries', 'SALT talks' and 'TUC Congress' are all technically redundant because the second word is already contained in the preceding abbreviation, but only the ultra-finicky would deplore them. Similarly in 'wipe that smile off your face' the last two words are tautological – there is no other place a smile could be – but the sentence would not stand without them.

On the whole, however, the use of more words than necessary is almost always better avoided, although it can be found even in the most respectable usage guides, as here: 'All writers and speakers of English, including these very grammarians themselves, omit words which will never be missed' (the Evanses in *A Dictionary of Contemporary American Usage*). '. . . these very grammarians themselves' is a patently redundant phrase. It should be either 'these grammarians themselves' or 'these very grammarians' but not a combination of the two.

Finally, *solecism* describes any violation of idiom or grammar. Redundancies, tautologies and pleonasms are all solecisms.

taxiing for the act of moving a plane into position.

Technicolor is a brand and company name and thus is both capitalized and spelled in the American manner.

Teesside. Possibly the most commonly misspelled geographical designation in Britain, as here: 'As the change of title indicates, the centre of gravity has moved several thousand miles westward from working-class Teeside to industrial New England' (*Independent*). Note -ss-.

temblor, not *trem-*, for an earthquake.

temperature. See FEVER, TEMPERATURE.

temporary respite. 'Even Saudi Arabia's assurance that it would not cut oil prices provided no more than a temporary respite' (*Daily Telegraph*). The expression is common, but redundant. A respite can only be temporary.

than. Three small but common problems need noting.

1. In comparative constructions *than* is often wrongly used, as here: 'Nearly twice as many people die under 20 in France than in Great Britain' (cited by Gowers). Make it 'as in Great Britain'.

2. It is wrongly used after 'hardly' in sentences such as this: 'Hardly had I landed at Liverpool than the Mikado's death recalled me to Japan' (cited by Fowler). Make it 'No sooner had I landed than' or 'Hardly had I landed when'.

3. It is often a source of ambiguity in sentences of the following type: 'She likes tennis more than me'. Does this mean that she likes tennis more than I do or that she likes tennis more than she likes me? In such cases, it is better to supply a second verb if it avoids ambiguity, e.g., 'She likes tennis more than she likes me' or 'She likes tennis more than I do'. Fowler provides a good example of ambiguity: 'I would rather you shot the poor dog than me'. (See also I, ME.)

that (as a conjunction). Whether you say 'I think you are wrong' or 'I think that you are wrong' is partly a matter of idiom but mostly a matter of preference. Some words usually require *that* (assert, contend, maintain) and some usually do not (say, think), but there are no hard rules. On the whole, it is better to dispense with *that* when it isn't necessary.

that, which. To understand the distinctions between *that* and *which* it is necessary to understand defining and non-defining clauses. Learning these distinctions is not, it must be said, anyone's idea of a good time, but it is one technical aspect of grammar that every professional user of English should understand because it is at the root of an assortment of grammatical errors.

A non-defining clause is one that can be regarded as parenthetical: 'The tree, *which had no leaves*, was a birch'. The italicized words are effectively an aside and could be deleted. The real point of the sentence is that the tree was a birch; its leaflessness is incidental. A defining clause is one that is essential to the sense of the sentence: 'The tree *that had no leaves* was a birch'. Here the leaflessness is a defining characteristic; it helps us to distinguish that tree from other trees.

In correct usage *that* is always used to indicate defining clauses and *which* to indicate non-defining ones. Defining clauses should never be set off with commas and non-defining clauses always should. On that much the authorities are agreed. Where divergence creeps in is on the question of how strictly the distinctions should be observed.

Until relatively recently they were not observed at all. In the King James Bible, for instance, we find: 'Render therefore unto Caesar the things which are Caesar's; and unto God the things that are God's'. The same quotation appears twice more in the Bible – once with *that* in both places and once with *which* in both. Today, *that* is more usual in short sentences or early on in longer ones ('The house that Jack built', 'The mouse that roared'). *Which* often appears where *that* would more strictly be correct, particularly in Britain, as here: 'It has outlined two broad strategies which it thinks could be put to the institutions' (*The Times*).

Although there is ample precedent for using *which* in defining clauses, the practice is on the whole better avoided. There are, at any rate, occasions when the choice of *which* is clearly wrong, as here: 'On a modest estimate, public authorities own 100,000 houses, which remain unoccupied for at least a year' (*Sunday Times*). What the writer meant was that of those houses that are publicly owned, at least 100,000 are left vacant for a year or more. Deleting the comma after 'houses' and changing *which* to *that* would have made this immediately clear.

Another common fault – more a discourtesy to the reader than an error – is the failure to set off non-defining clauses with commas, as here: 'Four members of one of the world's largest drugs rings (,) which smuggled heroin worth £5 million into Britain (,) were jailed yesterday' (*The Times*). That lapse is seen only rarely in America, but is rife in Britain; it occurred five times more in the same article.

Americans, on the other hand, are much more inclined to use *that* where *which* might be preferable, as here: 'Perhaps, with the help of discerning decision-makers, the verb can regain its narrow definition that gave it a reason for being' (Safire, *On Language*). Had Safire written 'can regain *the* narrow definition that gave it a reason for being', all would be well. But the use of 'its' gives the final clause the feel of a non-defining afterthought and the sentence might be better rendered as 'can regain its narrow definition, which gave it a reason for being'. The point is arguable.

'Their's not to reason why, / Their's but to do and die'. See 'OURS IS NOT TO REASON WHY, OURS IS BUT TO DO OR DIE'.

thinking to oneself. 'Somehow he must have thought to himself that this unfamiliar line needed to be ascribed to someone rather more venerable' (*Sunday Telegraph*); '"Can it be that the Sunday Times Magazine is paying no attention to my book?" Frank Delaney was thinking to himself' (*Sunday Times*). Scrub 'to himself' both times; there is no one else to whom you can think. Similarly vacuous is 'in my mind' here: 'I could picture in my mind where the bookkeeping offices had been' (*Boston Globe*).

though, although. The two are interchangeable except at the end of a sentence, where only *though* is correct ('He looked tired, though'), and with the expressions 'as though' and 'even though', where idiom precludes *although*.

Through the Looking-Glass and What Alice Found There is the full, formal title of the 1871 Lewis Carroll classic. Note the hyphen in *Looking-Glass*.

tic douloureux for the disorder of the facial nerves. Its formal medical designation is trigeminal neuralgia.

till. See UNTIL, TILL, 'TIL, 'TILL.

'til. See UNTIL, TILL, 'TIL, 'TILL.

'till. See UNTIL, TILL, 'TIL, 'TILL.

time. Often used superfluously in constructions of this sort: 'The report will be available in two weeks time' (*Guardian*). *Time* adds nothing to the sentence but length, and its deletion would obviate the need for an apostrophe after 'weeks'.

time, at this moment in. Unless you are striving for an air of linguistic ineptitude, never use this expression. Say 'now'.

tirade. See HARANGUE, TIRADE.

to all intents and purposes is a tautology. 'To all intents' is enough.

together with, along with. *With* in both expressions is a preposition, not a conjunction, and therefore does not govern the verb. This sentence is wrong: 'They said the man, a motor mechanic, together with a 22-year-old arrested a day earlier, were being questioned' (*The Times*). Make it 'was being questioned'.

A separate danger with such expressions is seen here: 'Barbara Tuchman, the historian, gave $20,000 to the Democrats, along with her husband, Lester' (*The New York Times*). How Lester felt about being given to the Democrats wasn't recorded.

ton, tonne. There are two kinds of ton: a *long ton* (used principally in the UK) weighing 2,240lb/1,016kg and a *short ton* (used in the US and Canada) weighing 2,000lb/907kg. A *tonne* is a metric ton and weighs 2,204lb/1,000kg.

tonnages of ships. *Deadweight tonnage* is the amount of cargo a ship can carry. *Displacement tonnage* is the weight of the ship itself. *Gross tonnage* measures the theoretical capacity of a ship based on its dimensions. When discussing ship tonnages, it is only fair to the reader to give some brief idea of what they signify.

tonne. See TON, TONNE.

tortuous, torturous. *Tortuous* means winding and circuitous ('The road wound tortuously through the mountains'). When used figuratively it usually suggests crookedness or deviousness ('a tortuous tax avoidance scheme'). The word is thus better avoided if all you mean is complicated or convoluted. *Torturous* is the adjectival form of *torture* and describes the infliction of extreme pain. It is the word that should have been used here: 'And only a tortuous number of repetitions could seriously increase your abdominal strength' (advertisement in *The New York Times*).

torturous. See TORTUOUS, TORTUROUS.

total. Three points to note:

1. *Total* is redundant and should be deleted when what it is qualifying already contains the idea of a totality, as here: '[They] risk total annihilation at the hands of the massive Israeli forces now poised to strike at the gates of the city' (*Washington Post*).

2. The expression *a total of*, though common, is also generally superfluous: 'County officials said a total of 84 prisoners were housed in six cells . . .' (*The New York Times*). Make it 'officials said 84 prisoners'. An exception is at the start of a sentence, when it is desirable to avoid spelling out a large number, as in 'A total of 2,112 sailors were aboard' instead of 'Two thousand one hundred and twelve sailors were aboard'.

3. 'A total of 45 weeks was spent on the study' (*The Times*) is wrong. As with 'a number of ' and 'the number of ', the rule is to make it 'the total of . . . was' but 'a total of . . . were'.

to the tune of. A hackneyed circumlocution. 'The company is being subsidized to the tune of $500 million a year' would be more succinct as 'The company is receiving a subsidy of $500 million a year'.

toward. See TOWARDS, TOWARD.

towards, toward. The first is the preferred form in Britain, the second in America, but either is correct. *Untoward*, however, is the only accepted form in both.

trade mark, trade name. A *trade mark* is a name, symbol or other depiction that formally identifies a product. A *trade name* is the name of the maker, not of the product. Cadillac is a trade mark, General Motors a trade name.

transatlantic. 'The agreement came just in time to stop the authorities from taking away his permits to operate trans-Atlantic flights' (*Sunday Times*). Most dictionaries prefer *transatlantic*. Similarly, *transalpine, transarctic, transpacific*.

translucent is sometimes wrongly treated as a synonym for 'transparent'. A translucent material is one through which light passes but through which images cannot be clearly seen, as with frosted glass. Note also the spelling: it is not *-scent*.

transpire. 'But Mayor Koch had a different version of what transpired' (*The New York Times*). *Transpire* does not mean occur, as was intended above. Still less does it mean arrive or be received, as was intended here: 'And generally the group found it had too many stocks for the orders that transpired' (*The Times*). It means to leak out (literally in Latin 'to breathe through') and is best reserved for that sense.

treble. See TRIPLE, TREBLE.

triple, treble. Either word can be used as a noun, verb or adjective. Except in certain musical senses ('treble clef'), *triple* is used almost exclusively for all three in America and is becoming increasingly preponderant in Britain. According to Fowler (second edition), *treble* is more usual as a verb ('They trebled their profits') and as a noun ('I will give you treble what he offered'). As an adjective, he says, *treble* is preferable for amount and *triple* for kinds. Burchfield, in the third edition, offers no guidance, but rather observes that as an adjective *treble* is perhaps 'more commonly used with amounts and triple with plurality, particularly with regard to things of three equal parts'. In short, use them as you will.

trivia is, strictly speaking, a plural, and many dictionaries only recognize it as such. 'All this daily trivia is getting on my nerves' should be 'All these daily trivia are getting on my nerves'. There is no singular form (the Latin *trivium* now has only historical applications), but there are the singular words *trifle* and *triviality*. The other option, if the plural form seems ungainly, is to convert *trivia* into an adjective: 'All these trivial daily matters are getting on my nerves'.

Trooping the Colour. The annual event celebrating the Queen's official birthday in June (as opposed to her actual birthday in April) is not Trooping of the Colour, still less the Trooping of the Colour, but just Trooping the Colour.

true facts. 'No one in the White House seems able to explain why it took such a potentially fatal time to inform the Vice President of the true facts' (*Sunday Times*). *True facts* is always either redundant or wrong. All facts are true. Things that are not true are not facts.

try and is colloquial and better avoided in serious writing. 'The Monopolies Commission will look closely at retailing mergers to try and prevent any lessening of competition' (*Sunday Times*). Make it 'try to prevent'.

tumult, turmoil. Both describe confusion and agitation. The difference is that *tumult* applies only to people, but *turmoil* applies to both people and things. *Tumultuous*, however, can also describe things as well as people (tumultuous applause, tumultuous seas).

turbid. See TURGID, TURBID.

turgid, turbid. It is seldom possible to tell with certainty whether a writer is using *turgid* in its proper sense or is confusing it with *turbid*, but confusion would appear to be the case here: 'She insisted on reading the entire turgid work aloud, a dusk-to-dawn affair that would have tried anyone's patience' (*Sunday Times*). *Turgid* means inflated, grandiloquent, bombastic. It does not mean muddy or impenetrable, which meanings are covered by *turbid*.

turmoil. See TUMULT, TURMOIL.

turpitude does not signify rectitude or integrity, as is sometimes thought, but rather baseness or depravity. 'He is a man of great moral turpitude' is not a compliment.

Tussaud's, Madame, for the London waxworks museum. The apostrophe is not optional.

U

UCLA. 'A professor of higher education at the University College of Los Angeles has examined the careers of 200,000 students at 350 colleges' (*Sunday Times*). The error is a common one outside North America. UCLA stands for the University of California at Los Angeles.

Uffizi Gallery, Florence.

ukulele for the stringed instrument. Not *uke-*.

Ullswater, Cumbria. Not *Uls-*.

Uluru is now the formal, and generally preferred, name for Ayers Rock in Australia. Pronounced *oo-luh-roo*. It is part of Uluru-Kata Tjuta National Park. The resort alongside it is Yulara.

undoubtedly. See DOUBTLESS, UNDOUBTEDLY, INDUBITABLY.

unexceptionable, unexceptional. Sometimes confused. Something that is unexceptional is ordinary, not outstanding ('an unexceptional wine'). Something that is unexceptionable is not open to objections ('In Britain, *grey* is the preferred spelling, but *gray* is unexceptionable').

unexceptional. See UNEXCEPTIONABLE, UNEXCEPTIONAL.

unilateral, bilateral, multilateral. All are often unneeded, as here: 'Bilateral trade talks are to take place next week between Britain and Japan' (*The Times*). Trade talks between Britain and Japan could hardly be other than two-sided. Delete *bilateral*.

uninterested. See DISINTERESTED, UNINTERESTED.

unique means the only one of its kind, something incomparable. One thing cannot be more unique than another, as was thought here: 'Lafayette's most unique restaurant is now even more unique' (cited by Wood).

unknown is often used imprecisely, as here: 'A hitherto unknown company called Ashdown Oil has emerged as a bidder for the Wytch Farm oil interests' (*The Times*). A company must be known to someone, if only its directors. It would be better to call it 'a little-known company'.

unless and until. One or the other, please.

unlike. When *unlike* is used as a preposition, it should govern a noun or pronoun or a noun equivalent (e.g., a gerund). 'But unlike at previous sessions of the conference . . .' (*The New York Times*) needs to be 'But unlike previous sessions' or 'As was not the case at previous sessions'.

Unlike must also contrast things that are comparable, which was not done here: 'Unlike the proposal by Rep. Albert Gore, outlined in this space yesterday, the President is not putting forth a blueprint for a final treaty' (*Chicago Tribune*). As written, the sentence is telling us that a proposal is unlike the President. It should be: 'Unlike the proposal by Rep. Albert Gore, the President's plan does not put forth a blueprint' or words to that effect.

unpractical. See IMPRACTICAL, IMPRACTICABLE, UNPRACTICAL.

until, till, 'til, 'till. The first two are legitimate and interchangeable. The second two are archaic.

untimely death is a common but really quite inane expression. When ever was a death timely?

up. When used as a phrasal verb (which see), *up* is often just a hitchhiker, joining sentences only for the ride. Occasionally idiom dictates that we include it: we look up a word in a book, we dig up facts, we move up in our careers. But often its appearance is entirely needless, as in these examples: 'Another time, another tiger ate up 27 of Henning's 30 prop animals' (*Washington Post*); 'Plans to tighten up the rules . . . of the National Health Service were announced yesterday' (*The Times*); 'This could force the banks to lift up their interest rates' (*Financial Times*). In these and countless other cases, *up* should be unceremoniously expunged. Occasionally in its eagerness *up* moves to the front of words: 'With the continued upsurge in sales of domestic appliances . . .' (*The Times*). Although 'upsurge' is a recognized word, it seldom means more than 'surge'.

upon. See ON, UPON.

usage. See USE, USAGE.

use, usage. *Usage* normally appears only in the context of formal practices, particularly in regard to linguistics ('modern English usage'), and *use* does duty for all other senses, but most dictionaries recognize the words as interchangeable in nearly all contexts.

usual. A common oversight in newspapers, no doubt attributable to haste, is telling readers twice in a sentence that a thing is customary. Both of the following are from *The New York Times*: 'The usual procedure normally involved getting eyewitness reports of one or more acts of heroism'; 'Customarily, such freezes are usually imposed at the end of a fiscal year'. Delete something. (See also HABITS.)

utilize. In its strictest sense, *utilize* means to make the best use of something that wasn't intended for the job ('He utilized a coat hanger to repair his car'). It can be legitimately extended to mean making the most practical use of something ('Although the hills were steep, the rice farmers utilized every square inch of the land'), but in all other senses 'use' is better.

V

Van Dyck, Vandyke. The seventeenth-century painter, whose name can be found variously spelled and misspelled, was born Anton Van Dijck, but that spelling is almost never encountered outside his native Belgium. In Britain his name is usually rendered as Sir Anthony Van Dyck, though Vandyke is also acceptable. Paintings by him are usually referred to as Vandykes, as are objects associated with him – e.g., a Vandyke beard, a Vandyke collar.

Vandyke. See VAN DYCK, VANDYKE.

various different is inescapably repetitive.

venal, venial. *Venial*, from the Latin *venialis* ('forgivable'), means excusable; a venial sin is a minor one. *Venal* means corruptible. It comes from the Latin *venalis* ('for sale') and describes someone who is capable of being bought.

venerate, worship. Although in figurative senses the words are interchangeable, in religious contexts *worship* should apply only to God. Roman Catholics, for instance, worship God but venerate saints.

venial. See VENAL, VENIAL.

ventricles for the heart valves. Not *ventricals*.

verbal. See ORAL, VERBAL.

vermilion for the colour. Not *-ll-*.

very should be made to pay its way in sentences. Too often it is used where it adds nothing to sense ('It was a very tragic death'), or is inserted in a futile effort to prop up a weak word that would be better replaced by something with more punch ('The play was very good').

via, meaning 'by way of', indicates the direction of a journey and not the means by which the journey is achieved. It is correct to say, 'We flew from London to Sydney via Singapore' but not 'We travelled to the islands via seaplane'.

viable. 'Such a system would mark a breakthrough in efforts to come up with a commercially viable replacement for internal-combustion engines' (*Newsweek*); 'I believe there is a viable market for the Samba Cabriolet in Britain' (*Mail on Sunday*). *Viable* does not mean feasible or workable or promising, senses in which it is frequently used. It means capable of independent existence, and its use really ought to be confined to that meaning. Even when it is correctly used, it tends to make the sentence read like a government document, as here: 'Doing nothing about the latter threatens the viability of the lakes and woodlands of the northeastern states' (*Chicago Tribune*). Deleting 'the viability of' would shorten the sentence without altering its sense.

vichyssoise for the soup. Note *-ss-*.

vicissitude for a change or variation. Although there is no compelling reason for it, the word is almost always used in the plural.

vitreous, vitriform. The first describes something made, or having the quality, of glass. The second means to have the appearance of glass.

vitriform. See VITREOUS, VITRIFORM.

vocal cords. See CHORD, CORD.

volcanology. See VULCANOLOGY, VOLCANOLOGY.

vortexes, vortices. For the plural of *vortex*, either is correct.

vortices. See VORTEXES, VORTICES.

vulcanology, volcanology. Both are the terms for the science of volcanoes. The first is the preferred British spelling, the second the preferred American one.

W

waiver, waver. The first is a relinquishment of a claim; the second means to hesitate.

Wal-Mart for the American stores group (but *Kmart* for its chief rival). The company's full name is Wal-Mart Stores Inc.

warn. 'British Rail warned that the snow was bound to have a serious effect on its service today' (*Daily Telegraph*). Until fairly recent times, *warn* was almost never used intransitively in Britain, as it has been above. That is to say, it needed an expressed personal object – the person or thing that was being warned. Thus, to satisfy tradition, the sentence above needs to be recast along the lines of 'British Rail warned passengers that . . .'.

These days the weight of usage is clearly on the side of accepting the intransitive, and I can find only one authority (*The Times Guide to English Style and Usage*) that argues against it with anything approaching conviction. Burchfield notes the change in common usage, but passes no view. In the United States the word has long been permitted with or without an object, and I suspect that is swiftly becoming the case in Britain. But for the moment to use the word without an expressed object in Britain is to run the slight risk of censure.

'Water, water, everywhere, / Nor any drop to drink' are the lines from the Samuel Taylor Coleridge poem *The Rime of the Ancient Mariner*.

waver. See WAIVER, WAVER.

Waverley Station, Edinburgh.

weather conditions. 'Freezing weather conditions will continue for the rest of the week' (*The Times*). Delete 'conditions'. Similarly tiresome is the American weather forecasters' fondness for 'activity', as in 'thunderstorm activity over the plains states'.

Weddell Sea, Antarctica.

Wedgwood china. Not *Wedge-*.

Weidenfeld & Nicolson for the publisher. Not *-field*, not *Nich-*.

Westmorland, not *-more-*, for the former English county.

West Virginia is one of the fifty US states. It is quite separate from its neighbour Virginia, from which it was carved in 1863. Its capital is Charleston, which is not to be confused with the more famous seaport city of Charleston, South Carolina.

Westward Ho!, Devon. Note exclamation mark and comma before Devon.

what at the head of a sentence is often a sign of an ill-composed statement. 'What has characterised her evidence – and indeed the entire case – is the constant name-dropping' (*Sunday Times*) would be shorter and more active as 'Her evidence – and indeed the entire case – has been characterised by constant name-dropping'.

whence. 'And man will return to the state of hydrogen from whence he came' (*Sunday Telegraph*). Although there is ample precedent for *from whence* – the King James Bible has the sentence 'I will lift up my eyes unto the hills from whence cometh my help' – it is none the less tautological. *Whence* means 'from where'. It is enough to say 'to the state of hydrogen whence he came'.

whether or not. The second two words should be dropped when *whether* is equivalent to 'if', as here: 'It is not yet known whether or not persons who become reinfected can spread the virus to other susceptible individuals' (*The New York Times*). *Or not* is necessary, however, when what is being stressed is an alternative: 'I intend to come whether or not you like it'.

whet one's appetite. Not *wet*. The word has nothing to do with heightened salivary flow or anything of the like. It comes from an old English word, *hwettan*, meaning 'sharpen'. Hence also *whetstone*, for a stone used to sharpen knives.

which. The belief that *which* may refer only to the preceding word and not to the whole of a preceding statement is without foundation except where there is a chance of ambiguity. The impossibility of enforcing the rule consistently is illustrated by an anecdote cited by Gowers. A class in Philadelphia had written to a local paper's resident usage expert asking him what was wrong with the sentence 'He wrecked the car, which was due to his carelessness'. Notice how the authority hoists himself with the last three words of his reply: 'The fault lies in using *which* to refer to the statement "He wrecked the car". When *which* follows a noun, it refers to that noun as its antecedent. Therefore in the foregoing sentence it is stated that the car was due to his carelessness, which is nonsense'. (See also THAT, WHICH.)

whitish for the colour. Not *white-*.

whiz kid, not *whizz*, is generally the preferred spelling, though most dictionaries recognize both. The same applies for *whiz-bang*, but with the addition of a hyphen.

who, whom. For those who are perennially baffled by the distinction between these two relative pronouns, it may come as some comfort to know that Shakespeare, Addison, Ben Jonson, Dickens, Churchill and the translators of the King James Bible have equally been flummoxed in their time.

The rule can be stated simply. *Whom* is used when it is the object of a preposition ('To whom it may concern') or verb ('The man whom we saw last night') or the subject of a complementary infinitive ('The person whom we took to be your father'). *Who* is used on all other occasions.

Consider now three extracts in which the wrong choice has been made: 'Mrs Hinckley said that her son had been upset by the murder of Mr Lennon, who he idolized' (*The New York Times*); 'Colombo, whom law enforcement officials have said is the head of a Mafia family in Brooklyn . . .' (*The New York Times*); 'Heart-breaking decision – who to save' (*Times* headline). We can check the correctness of such sentences by imagining them as he/him constructions. For instance, would you say that 'Hinckley idolized he' or 'idolized him'? Would law enforcement officers say that 'he is the head of a Mafia family' or 'him is the head'? And is it a heart-breaking decision over whether to save he or to save him?

Simple, isn't it? Well, not quite. When the relative pronoun follows a preposition in a relative clause, the simple test falls to pieces. Consider this sentence from *Fortune* magazine: 'They rent it to whomever needs it'. Since we know that you say 'for whom the bell tolls' and 'to whom it may concern', it should follow that we would say 'to whomever needs it'. If we test that conclusion by imagining the sentence as a he/him construction – would they 'rent it to he' or 'rent it to him'? – we are bound to plump for *whom*. But we would be wrong. The difficulty is that the relative pronoun is the subject of the verb 'needs' and the object of the preposition 'to'. The sentence in effect is saying: 'They rent it to any person who needs it'.

Similarly, *whomever* would be wrong in these two sentences: 'We must offer it to whoever applies first'; 'Give it to whoever wants it'. Again, in effect they are saying: 'We must offer it to the person who applies first' and 'Give it to the person who wants it'.

Such constructions usually involve a choice between *whoever* and *whomever* (as opposed to a simple *who* and *whom*), which should always alert you to proceed with caution, but they need not. An exception – and a rather tricky one – is seen here: 'The disputants differed diametrically as to who they thought might turn out to be the violator' (cited by Bernstein). The sentence is saying: 'The disputants differed diametrically as to the identity of the person who, they thought, might turn out to be the violator'.

Most sentences, it must be said, are much more straightforward than this, and by performing a little verbal gymnastics it is usually possible to decide with some confidence which case to use. But is it worth the bother? Bernstein, in his later years, thought not. In 1975, he wrote to twenty-five authorities on usage asking if they thought there was any real point in preserving *whom* except when it is directly governed by a preposition (as in 'to whom it may concern'). Six voted to preserve *whom*, four were undecided and fifteen thought it should be abandoned.

English has been shedding its pronoun declensions for hundreds of years; today *who* is the only relative pronoun that is still declinable. Preserving the distinction between *who* and *whom* does nothing to promote clarity or reduce ambiguity. It has become merely a source of frequent errors and perpetual uncertainty. Authorities have been tossing stones at *whom* for at least 200 years – Noah Webster was one of the first to call it needless – but the word refuses to go away. A century from now it may be a relic, but for the moment you ignore it at the risk of being thought unrefined. And there is, in my view, a certain elegance in seeing a tricky *whom* properly applied. I, for one, would not like to see it go.

whodunit is the usual spelling for a mystery story. Note the single 'n'.

whom. See WHO, WHOM.

whose. Two small problems here. One is the persistent belief that *whose* can apply only to people. The authorities are unanimous that there is nothing wrong with saying, 'The book, a picaresque novel whose central characters are . . .' rather than the clumsier 'a picaresque novel the central characters of which are . . .'.

The second problem arises from a failure to discriminate between defining and non-defining clauses (discussed under THAT, WHICH). Consider: 'Many parents, whose children ride motorbikes, live in constant fear of an accident' (*Observer*). By making the subordinate clause parenthetical (i.e., setting it off with commas) the writer is saying in effect: 'Many parents live in constant fear of an accident and by the way their children ride motorbikes'. The writer meant, of course, that the parents live in fear because their children ride motorbikes; that notion is not incidental to the full thought. Thus the clause is defining and the commas should be removed. Gowers cites this example from a wartime training manual: 'Pilots, whose minds are dull, do not usually live long'. Removing the commas would convert an insult into sound advice.

The same problem often happens with *who*, as in this sentence from my old style book at *The Times*: 'Normalcy should be left to the Americans who coined it'. Had the writer meant that 'normalcy' should be left only to those Americans who participated in its coining, the absence of a comma would be correct. However, we must assume he meant that it should be left to all Americans, who as a nation, and as an incidental matter, coined it. A comma is therefore required. (In fact, we didn't coin the word. It is several hundred years older than the United States and belongs to the English, who coined it. See NORMALCY.)

widow, when combined with 'the late', is always redundant, as here: 'Mrs Sadat, the widow of the late Egyptian President . . .' (*Guardian*). Make it either 'wife of the late Egyptian President' or 'widow of the Egyptian President'.

will, would. 'The plan would be phased in over 10 years and will involve extra national insurance contributions . . .' (*The Times*). The problem here is an inconsistency between what grammarians call the protasis (the condition) and the apodosis (the consequence). The sentence has begun in the subjunctive (*would*) and switched abruptly to the indicative (*will*). The same error occurs here: 'The rector, Chad Varah, has promised that work on the church will start in the New Year and would be completed within about three years' (*Standard*). In both sentences it should be either *will* both times or *would* both times.

This is not simply a matter of grammatical orderliness. It is a question of clarity – of telling the difference between what may happen and what will happen. If you write, 'The plan will cost £400 million', you are expressing a certainty. The plan either has been adopted or is certain to be adopted. If you write, 'The plan would cost £400 million', the statement is clearly suppositional. It is saying only that if the plan were adopted it would cost £400 million.

A common failing in British journalism is to present the suppositional as if it were a certainty. An article in the *Guardian* about union proposals urging the Prime Minister to spend more on job creation schemes went on to say: 'The proposals will create up to 20,000 new jobs . . . will be phased in over three years . . . will cost up to £8 million' and so on. In each instance the thought should be qualified: 'The proposals *would* create up to 20,000 jobs' or 'If they are adopted, the proposals *will* cost up to £8 million'.

For additional problems with *will*, see SHALL, WILL.

Wilshire Boulevard for the street in Los Angeles. Not *Wilt-*.

wistaria, wisteria. The plant was named for an anatomist named Caspar Wistar and some authorities therefore insist on the spelling *wistaria*. However, almost no dictionary supports this position and the formal genus spelling of the plant is *Wisteria*. Finally, but not least, Wistar sometimes spelled his name Wister.

wisteria. See WISTARIA, WISTERIA.

withheld. See WITHHOLD, WITHHELD.

withhold, withheld. Note -*hh*-.

women's. See MEN'S, WOMEN'S; POSSESSIVES.

wondrous. Not -*erous*.

Woolloomooloo for the district of Sydney, Australia. Note the single 'l' at the end.

World Bank. Officially it is the International Bank for Reconstruction and Development, but this title is rarely used, even on first reference.

World Court. Officially it is the International Court of Justice and that title should generally be used on first reference or soon thereafter.

worship. See VENERATE, WORSHIP.

worsted fabric. Not -*stead*.

would. See WILL, WOULD.

wound, scar. The two are not as interchangeable as writers sometimes casually make them. A scar is what remains after a wound heals. Thus it is always wrong, or at least stretching matters, to talk about a scar healing, including in figurative senses.

wrack. See RACK, WRACK.

wrapped. See RAPT, WRAPPED.

wunderkind, not *wonder*-, for a prodigy.

Y

year. A common error concerning the word *year* is seen here: 'The car that crossed the Channel, survived hippiedom and outlasted a million careful owners has reached its fiftieth year' (*Sunday Times*). The article, about the Citroën Deux Chevaux, was written on the occasion of the car's fiftieth anniversary; it had therefore reached its fifty-first year. As a moment's thought will confirm, you are always one year ahead of your age in the sense of what year you are in: a newborn infant is in his first year; after his birthday, he will be in his second year, and so on. The sentence should have said either that the car had completed its fiftieth year or reached its fifty-first.

years' time. 'In 1865 an influential book by Stanley Jevons argued ... that Britain would run out of coal in a few years' time' (*Economist*). The author is to be commended for putting an apostrophe on *years*, but the effort was unnecessary as pairing *time* with *years* is inescapably redundant. 'In a few short years' says as much and gets there quicker.

yes, no. Writers are often at a loss when deciding what to do with a *yes* or *no* in constructions such as the following: 'Will this really be the last of Inspector Clousseau? Blake Edwards says No' (*Sunday Express*). There are two possibilities, neither of which the writer has used. You may make it 'Blake Edwards says no' or you may make it 'Blake Edwards says, "No"'. Capitalizing the word without providing any punctuation is a pointless compromise and should satisfy no one.

yesterday. Anyone not acquainted with journalists could be forgiven for assuming that they must talk something like this: 'I last night went to bed early because I this morning had to catch an early flight'. That, at any rate, is how many of them write. Consider: 'Their decision was yesterday being heralded as a powerful warning . . .' (*The Times*); 'Police were last night hunting for . . .' (*Daily Mail*); 'The two sides were today to consider . . .' (*Guardian*). Although in newspapers care must be taken not to place the time element in a position where it might produce ambiguity, a more natural arrangement can almost always be found: 'was being heralded yesterday'; 'were hunting last night for'; 'were to consider today'.

Yiddish. See HEBREW, YIDDISH.

Z

zoom. Strictly speaking, the word should describe only a steep upward movement. Almost every authority stresses the point, though how much that is inspired by a desire for precision and how much by the need to find something – anything – to discuss under the letter 'Z' is not easy to say. No one, I think, would argue that zoom lenses should be used only for taking pictures of objects above oneself, nor should the word be considered objectionable when applied to lateral movements ('The cars zoomed around the track'). But for describing downward movements ('The planes zoomed down on the city to drop their bombs') it is perhaps better avoided, especially as 'swoop' is available.

Appendix: Punctuation

The uses of punctuation marks, or stops, are so numerous and the abuses so varied that the following is offered only as a very general guide to the most common errors. For those who wish to dig more deeply, I recommend the excellent *Mind the Stop* by G. V. Carey.

apostrophe. The principal functions of the apostrophe are to indicate omitted letters (*don't, can't, wouldn't*) and to show the possessive (strictly, the genitive) case (*John's book, the bank's money, the people's choice*).

In its more general uses the apostrophe normally causes little trouble to educated writers. But among advertisers it is endlessly, maddeningly, distressingly neglected. I have before me a holiday brochure offering 'This years holidays at last years prices'. 'Todays Tesco' offers its customers 'mens clothes', 'womens clothes' and 'childrens clothes'. In one thinnish Sunday supplement, nine advertisers clocked up fourteen such errors between them. The mistake is inexcusable and those who make it are linguistic Neandertals.

Two other types of error occur with some frequency and are worth noting. They involve:

1. *Multiple possessives.* This problem can be seen here: 'This is a sequel to Jeremy Paul's and Alan Gibson's play . . .' (*The Times*). The question is whether both of the apostrophes are necessary, and the answer in this instance is no. Because the reference is to a single play written jointly, only the second-named man needs to be in the possessive. Thus it should be: 'Jeremy Paul and Alan Gibson's play'. If the reference were to two or more plays written separately, both names would have to carry apostrophes. The rule

is that when possession is held in common, only the nearer antecedent should be possessive; when possession is separate, each antecedent must be in the possessive.

2. *Plural units of measure.* Many writers who would never think of omitting the apostrophes in 'a fair day's pay for a fair day's work' often do exactly that when the unit of measure is increased. Consider: 'Laker gets further 30 days credit' (*Times* headline); 'Mr Taranto, who had 30 years service with the company . . .' (*The New York Times*). Both 'days' and 'years' should carry an apostrophe. Alternatively we could insert an 'of' after the time elements ('30 days of credit', '19 years of service'). One or the other is necessary.

The problem is often aggravated by the inclusion of unnecessary words, as in each of these examples: 'The scheme could well be appropriate in 25 years time, he said' (*The Times*); 'Many diplomats are anxious to settle the job by the end of the session in two weeks time' (*Observer*); 'The Government is prepared to part with several hundred acres worth of property' (*Time*). Each requires an apostrophe. But that need could be obviated by excluding the superfluous wordage. What is 'in 25 years' time' if not 'in 25 years'? What does 'several hundred acres' worth of property' say that 'several hundred acres' does not?

colon. The colon marks a formal introduction or indicates the start of a series. A colon should not separate a verb from its object in simple enumerations. Thus it would be wrong to say: 'The four states bordering Texas are: New Mexico, Arkansas, Oklahoma and Louisiana'. The colon should be removed. But it would be correct to say: 'Texas is bordered by four states: New Mexico, Arkansas, Oklahoma and Louisiana'.

comma. The trend these days is to use the comma as sparingly as form and clarity allow. But there are certain instances in which it should appear but all too often does not. Equally, it has a tendency to crop up with alarming regularity in places where it has no business. It is, in short, the most abused of punctuation marks and one of the worst offenders of any kind in the English language. Essentially there are three situations where the comma's use is compulsory and a fourth where it is recommended.

1. *When the information provided is clearly parenthetical.* Consider these two sentences, both of which are correctly punctuated: 'Mr Lawson, the Energy Secretary, was unavailable for comment'; 'The ambassador, who arrived in Britain two days ago, yesterday met with the Prime Minister'. In both sentences, the information between the commas is incidental to the main thought. You could remove it and the sentence would still make sense. In the following examples, the writer has failed to set off the parenthetical information. I have provided slashes (the proper name, incidentally, is virgules) to show where the commas should have gone: 'British cars/says a survey/are more reliable than their foreign counterparts' (leader in the *Standard*); 'The New AT&T Tower on Madison Avenue/the first of a new breed/will be ready by the end of 1982' (*Sunday Times*); 'Operating mainly from the presidential palace at Baabda/southeast of Beirut, Habib negotiated over a 65-day period' (*Time*); 'Mary Chatillon, director of the Massachusetts General Hospital's Reading Language Disorder Unit/maintains: "It would simply appear to be . . ."' (*Time*). It should perhaps be noted that failure to put in a comma is particularly common after a parenthesis, as here: 'Mr James Grant, executive director of the United Nations Children's Fund (UNICEF)/ says . . .' (*The Times*).

Occasionally the writer recognizes that the sentence contains a parenthetical thought, but fails to discern just how much of the information is incidental, as here: 'At nine she won a scholarship to Millfield, the private school, for bright children of the rich' (*Standard*). If we removed what has been presented as parenthetical, the sentence would say: 'At nine she won a scholarship to Millfield for bright children'. There should be no comma after 'school' because the whole of the last statement is parenthetical.

A rarer error is seen here: 'But its big worry is the growing evidence that such ostentatious cars, the cheapest costs £55,240, are becoming socially unacceptable' (*The Times*). When the incidental information could stand alone as a sentence, it needs to be set off with stronger punctuation – either dashes or parentheses.

2. *When the information is non-defining.* The problem here – which is really much the same as that discussed in the previous three paragraphs – is illustrated by this incorrectly punctuated sentence from the *Daily Mail*: 'Cable TV would be socially divisive, the chairman of the BBC George Howard claimed last night'. The writer has failed to understand the distinction between (1) 'BBC chairman George Howard claimed last night' and (2) 'The chairman of the BBC, George Howard, claimed last night'. In (1), the name George Howard is essential to the sense of the sentence; it defines it. If we removed it, the sentence would say: 'BBC chairman claimed last night'. In (2), however, the name is non-defining. In effect it is parenthetical. We could remove it without altering the sense of the sentence: 'The chairman of the BBC claimed last night'. When a name or title can be removed, it should be set off with commas. When it cannot be removed, the use of commas is wrong.

Two hypothetical examples may help to clarify the distinction. Both are correctly punctuated. 'John Fowles's novel *The Collector* was a bestseller'; 'John Fowles's first novel, *The Collector*, was a bestseller'. In the first example the name of the novel is defining because *The Collector* is only one of several novels by Fowles. In the second example it is non-defining because only one novel can be the author's first one. We could delete *The Collector* from the second example without spoiling the sense of the sentence, but not from the first.

When something is the only one of its kind, it should be set off with commas; when it is only one of several, the use of commas is wrong. Thus these two sentences, both from *The Times*, are incorrect: 'When the well-known British firm, Imperial Metal Industries, developed two new types of superconducting wires . . .'; 'The writer in the American magazine, *Horizon*, was aware of this pretentiousness . . .'. The first example would be correct only if Imperial Metal Industries were the only well-known British firm, and the second would be correct only if *Horizon* were

America's only magazine. The same error in reverse occurs here: 'Julie Christie knows that in the week her new film *The Return of the Soldier* has opened . . .' (*Sunday Times*). Since *The Return of the Soldier* was Julie Christie's only new film of the week, it should have been set off with commas.

The error frequently occurs when a marriage partner is named: 'Mrs Thatcher and her husband Denis left London yesterday' (*Observer*). Since Mrs Thatcher has only one husband, it should be 'and her husband, Denis, left London yesterday'.

3. *With forms of address.* When addressing people, commas are obligatory around the names or titles of those addressed. 'Hit him Jim, hit him' (*Sunday Times*) should be 'Hit him, Jim, hit him'. The BBC television series *Yes Minister* should have been *Yes, Minister.* The film *I'm All Right Jack* should have been *I'm All Right, Jack.* The lack of a comma or commas is always sloppy and occasionally ambiguous. In 1981, for instance, the *Sunday Express* illustrated a novel serialization with the heading 'I'm choking Mr Herriot' when what it meant was 'I'm choking, Mr Herriot' – quite another matter.

4. *With interpolated words or phrases.* Words such as *moreover, meanwhile* and *nevertheless* and phrases such as *for instance* and *for example* traditionally have taken commas, but the practice has become increasingly discretionary over the years. In Britain they have been more freely abandoned than in America; Fowler, for instance, seldom used them. I would recommend using them when they suggest a pause or when ambiguity might result. This is especially true of *however.* Consider these two sentences: 'However hard he tried, he failed'; 'However, he tried hard, but failed'. To keep from confusing the reader, if only momentarily, it is a good idea to set off *however* with commas when it is used as an interpolation. Much the same could be said of *say*: 'She should choose a British Government stock with (,) say (,) five years to run' (*Daily Mail*).

dash. Dashes should be used in pairs to enclose parenthetical matter or singly to indicate a sharp break in a sentence ('I can't see a damn thing in here – ouch!') or to place emphasis on a point ('There are only two things we can count on – death and taxes'). Dashes are most effective when used sparingly and there should never be more than one pair in a single sentence. Fowler insists that when dashes are used in pairs, any punctuation interrupted by the first dash should be picked up after the second (e.g., 'If this is true – and no one can be sure that it is –, we should do something'). But on this, as with so much else to do with punctuation, Fowler is at odds with almost everyone else. There are two common errors with dashes:

1. Failing to mark the end of a parenthetical comment with a second dash: 'The group – it is the largest in its sector, with subsidiaries or associates in 11 countries, says trading has improved in the current year' (*The Times*). Make it 'countries – says'.

2. Allowing a word or phrase from the main part of the sentence to become locked within the parenthetical area, as here: 'There is another institution which appears to have an even more – shall we say, relaxed – attitude to security' (*The Times*). Removing the words between the dashes would give us an institution with 'an even more attitude'. *Relaxed* belongs to the sentence proper and needs to be put outside the dashes: 'There is another institution which appears to have an even more – shall we say? – relaxed attitude to security'. (See also PARENTHESES.)

ellipsis. An ellipsis (sometimes called an ellipse) is used to indicate that material has been omitted. It consists of three full stops (. . .) and not, as some writers think, a random scattering of them. When an ellipsis occurs at the end of a sentence, a fourth full stop is normally added.

exclamation marks are used to show strong emotion ('Get out!') or urgency ('Help me!'). They should almost never be used for giving emphasis to a simple statement of fact: 'It was bound to happen sometime! A bull got into a china shop here' (cited by Bernstein).

full stop (US, period). There are two common errors associated with the full stop, both of which arise from its absence. The first is the run-on sentence (that is, the linking of two complete thoughts by a comma). It is never possible to say when a run-on sentence is attributable to ignorance on the part of the writer or to whimsy on the part of the typesetter, but the error occurs frequently enough that ignorance must play a part. In each of the following I have indicated with a stroke where one sentence should end and the next should begin: 'Although GEC handled the initial contract, much of the equipment is American,/the computers and laser printers come from Hewlett Packard' (*Guardian*); 'Confidence is growing that Opec will resolve its crisis,/however the Treasury is drawing up contingency plans' (*The Times*); 'Funds received in this way go towards the cost of electricity and water supply,/industries, shops and communes pay higher rates' (*The Times*).

The second lapse arises when a writer tries to say too much in a single sentence, as here: 'The measures would include plans to boost investment for self-financing in industry, coupled with schemes to promote investment and saving, alleviate youth unemployment, fight inflation and lower budget deficits, as well as a new look at the controversial issue of reducing working hours' (*The Times*). If the writer has not lost his readers, he has certainly lost himself. The last lumbering flourish ('as well as a new look . . .') is grammatically unconnected to what has gone before; it just hangs there. The sentence is crying out for a full stop – almost anywhere would do – to give the reader a chance to absorb the wealth of information being provided.

Here is another in which the writer tells us everything but his phone number: 'But after they had rejected once more the umpires' proposals of $5,000 a man for the playoffs and $10,000 for the World Series on a three-year contract and the umpires had turned down a proposal of $3,000 for the playoffs and $7,000 for the World Series on a one-year contract, baseball leaders said the playoffs would begin today and they had umpires to man the games' (*The New York Times*).

There is no quota on full stops. When an idea is complicated, break it up and present it in digestible chunks. One idea to a sentence is still the best advice that anyone has ever given on writing.

hyphen. Almost nothing can be said with finality about the hyphen. As Fowler says, 'its infinite variety defies description'. Even the word for using a hyphen is contentious: some authorities hyphenate words, but others hyphen them. The principal function of the hyphen is to reduce the chances of ambiguity. Consider, for instance, the distinction between 'the 20-odd members of his Cabinet' and 'the 20 odd members of his Cabinet'. It is sometimes used to indicate pronunciation (de-ice), but not always (coalesce, reissue). Composite adjectives used before a noun are usually given hyphens (a six-foot-high wall, a four-inch rainfall), but again not always. Fowler cites 'a balance-of-payments deficit' and Gowers 'a first-class ticket', but in expressions such as these, where the words are frequently linked, the hyphens are no more necessary than they would be in 'a trade-union conference' or 'a Post-Office strike'. When the phrases are used adverbially, the use of hyphens is wrong, as here: 'Mr Conran, who will be 50-years-old next month . . .' (*Sunday Times*). Mr Conran will be 50 years old next month; he will then be a 50-year-old man.

In general, hyphens should be dispensed with when they are not necessary. One place where they are not required by sense but frequently occur anyway is with '-ly' adverbs, as in 'newly-elected' or 'widely-held'. Almost every authority suggests that they should be deleted in such constructions.

parentheses. Parenthetical matter can be thought of as any information so incidental to the main thought that it needs to be separated from the sentence that contains it. It can be set off with dashes, brackets (usually reserved for explanatory insertions in quotations), commas or, of course, parentheses. It is, in short, an insertion and has no grammatical effect on the sentence in which it appears. It is rather as if the sentence does not even know it is there. Thus this statement from *The Times* is incorrect: 'But that is not how Mrs Graham (and her father before her) have made a success of the *Washington Post*'. The verb should be 'has'.

But while the parenthetical expression has no grammatical effect on the sentence in which it appears, the sentence does influence the parenthesis. Consider this extract from the *Los Angeles Times* (which, although it uses dashes, could equally have employed parentheses): 'One reason for the dearth of Japanese-American politicians is that no Japanese immigrants were allowed to become citizens – and thus could not vote – until 1952'. As written the sentence is telling us that 'no Japanese citizens could not vote'. Delete 'could not'.

When a parenthetical comment is part of a larger sentence, the full stop should appear after the second parenthesis (as here). (But when the entire sentence is parenthetical, as here, the full stop should appear inside the final parenthesis.)

question mark. The question mark comes at the end of a question. That sounds simple enough, doesn't it? But it's astonishing how frequently writers fail to include it. Two random examples: ' "Why travel all the way there when you could watch the whole thing at home," he asked' (*The Times*); 'The inspector got up to go and stood on Mr Ellis's cat, killing it. "What else do you expect from these people," said the artist' (*Standard*).

Occasionally question marks are included when they are not called for, as in this sentence by Trollope, cited by Fowler: 'But let me ask of her enemies whether it is not as good a method as any other known to be extant?' The problem here is a failure to distinguish between a direct question and an indirect one. Direct questions always take question marks: 'Who is going with you?' Indirect questions never do: 'I would like to know who is going with you'.

When direct questions take on the tone of a command, the use of a question mark becomes more discretionary. 'Will everyone please assemble in my office at four o'clock?' is strictly correct, but not all authorities insist on the question mark there.

A less frequent problem arises when a direct question appears outside a direct quotation. Fieldhouse, in *Everyman's Good English Guide*, suggests that the following punctuation is correct: 'Why does this happen to us, we wonder?' The Fowler brothers, however, call this an amusing blunder; certainly it is extremely irregular. The more usual course is to attach the question mark directly to the question. Thus: 'Why does this happen to us? we wonder'. But such constructions are clumsy and are almost always improved by being turned into indirect questions: 'We wonder why this happens to us'.

quotation marks (inverted commas). An issue that arises frequently in Britain, but almost never in America, is whether to put full stops and other punctuation inside or outside quotation marks when they appear together. The practice that prevails almost exclusively in America and is increasingly common in Britain is to put the punctuation inside the quotes. Thus: 'He said: "I will not go."' But some publishers prefer the punctuation to fall outside except when it is part of the quotation. Thus the example above would be: 'He said: "I will not go".'

Both systems are marked by inconsistencies – even Americans are forced to put the punctuation outside the quotes in such sentences as 'Which of you said, "Look out"?' – and there is not much to choose between them on grounds of logic. Similarly, the question of whether to use single quotes (') or double quotes (") is entirely a matter of preference except when it is dictated by house-style.

When quotation marks are used to set off a complete statement, the first word of the quotation should be capitalized ('He said, "Victory is ours"') except when the quotation is preceded by 'that' ('He said that "victory is ours"'). Fowler believed that no punctuation was necessary to set off attributive quotations; he would, for instance, delete the commas from the following: 'Tomorrow', he said, 'is a new day'. His argument was that commas are not needed to mark the interruption or introduction of a quotation because the quotation marks already do that. Logically he is correct. But with equal logic we could argue that question marks should be dispensed with on the grounds that the context almost always makes it clear that a question is being asked. The commas are required not by logic but by convention.

semicolon. The semicolon is heavier than the comma but lighter than the full stop. Its principal function is to divide contact clauses – that is, two ideas that are linked by sense but that lack a conjunction. For instance: 'You take the high road; I'll take the low road'. Equally that could be made into two complete sentences or, by introducing a conjunction, into one ('You take the high road and I'll take the low road'). The semicolon is also sometimes used to separate long coordinate clauses. In this role it was formerly used much more extensively than it is today – Fowler, for instance, would often string together a whole series of semicolons. Today its use is almost entirely discretionary. Many good writers scarcely use the semicolon at all.

Bibliography

Throughout the text I have in general referred to the following books by the surname of the author, ignoring the contributions of those who revised the originals. Thus although Sir Ernest Gowers substantially revised *A Dictionary of Modern English Usage* in 1965, that book is referred to throughout the text as 'Fowler'. References to 'Gowers' are meant to suggest Gowers's own book, *The Complete Plain Words*.

Aitchison, Jean, *Language Change: Progress or Decay?*, Fontana, London, 1981.

American Heritage Dictionary, American Heritage Publishing Company, New York, 1969.

Bernstein, Theodore M., *The Careful Writer*, Atheneum, New York, 1967.
  Dos, Don'ts and Maybes of English Usage, Times Books, New York, 1977.

Burchfield, R. W. (ed.), *The New Fowler's Modern Usage* (third edition), Clarendon Press, Oxford, 1996.

Carey, G. V., *Mind the Stop*, Penguin, Harmondsworth, 1971.

Collins Dictionary of the English Language, Collins, London, 1979.

Concise Oxford Dictionary of Current English, Oxford University Press, Oxford, 1982.

Crystal, David, *Who Cares About English Usage?*, Penguin, Harmondsworth, 1985.

Encarta World English Dictionary, Bloomsbury, London, 1999.

Evans, Bergen and Cornelia, *A Dictionary of Contemporary American Usage*, Random House, New York, 1957.

Fieldhouse, Harry, *Everyman's Good English Guide*, J. M. Dent & Sons, London, 1982.

Fowler, E. G. and H. W., *The King's English*, third edition, Oxford University Press, London, 1970.

Fowler, H. W., *A Dictionary of Modern English Usage*, second edition (revised by Sir Ernest Gowers), Oxford University Press, Oxford, 1980.

Gowers, Sir Ernest, *The Complete Plain Words*, second edition (revised by Sir Bruce Fraser), Penguin, Harmondsworth, 1980.

Grimond, John, *The Economist Pocket Style Book*, Economist Publications, London, 1986.

Howard, Philip, *Weasel Words*, Hamish Hamilton, London, 1978.
New Words for Old, Unwin, London, 1980.
Words Fail Me, Hamish Hamilton, London, 1980.
A Word in Your Ear, Penguin, Harmondsworth, 1985.
The State of the Language, Penguin, Harmondsworth, 1986.

Hudson, Kenneth, *The Dictionary of Diseased English*, Papermac, London, 1980.

Jordan, Lewis (ed.), *The New York Times Manual of Style and Usage*, Times Books, New York, 1976.

Michaels, Leonard, and Ricks, Christopher (ed.), *The State of the Language*, University of California Press, Berkeley, 1980.

Morris, William and Mary, *Harper Dictionary of Contemporary Usage*, Harper & Row, New York, 1975.

Newman, Edwin, *Strictly Speaking*, Warner Books, New York, 1975.
A Civil Tongue, Warner Books, New York, 1976.

Onions, C. T., *Modern English Syntax*, seventh edition (prepared by B. D. H. Miller), Routledge & Kegan Paul, London, 1971.

Oxford Dictionary for Writers and Editors, Oxford University Press, Oxford, 1981.

Oxford Dictionary of English Etymology, Oxford University Press, Oxford, 1982.

Oxford English, Guild Publishing, London, 1986.

Oxford English Dictionary (Compact Edition), Oxford University Press, Oxford, 1971.

Oxford Guide to the English Language, Guild Publishing, London, 1984.

Palmer, Frank, *Grammar*, Penguin, Harmondsworth, 1982.

Partridge, Eric, *Usage and Abusage*, fifth edition, Penguin, Harmondsworth, 1981.

Phythian, B. A., *A Concise Dictionary of Correct English*, Hodder & Stoughton, London, 1979.

Potter, Simeon, *Our Language*, Penguin, Harmondsworth, 1982.

Quirk, Randolph, *The Use of English*, Longmans, London, 1969.

Safire, William, *On Language*, Avon, New York, 1980.

　What's the Good Word?, Times Books, New York, 1982.

Shaw, Harry, *Dictionary of Problem Words and Expressions*, McGraw-Hill, New York, 1975.

Shipley, Joseph T., *In Praise of English: The Growth and Use of Language*, Times Books, New York, 1977.

Shorter Oxford English Dictionary, Book Club Associates, London, 1983.

Simon, John, *Paradigms Lost: Reflections on Literacy and Its Decline*, Clarkson N. Potter, New York, 1980.

Strunk Jr, William, and White, E. B., *The Elements of Style*, third edition, Macmillan, New York, 1979.

Wood, Frederick T., *Current English Usage*, Papermac, London, second edition (revised by R. H. and L. M. Flavell), 1981.

Glossary

Grammatical terms are, to quote Frank Palmer, 'largely notional and often extremely vague'. In 'I went swimming', for instance, *swimming* is a present participle; but in 'Swimming is good for you', it is a gerund. Because such distinctions are for many of us a source of continuing perplexity, I have tried to use most such terms sparingly throughout the book. Inevitably, however, they do sometimes appear, and the following is offered as a simple guide for those who are confused or need refreshing. For a fuller discussion, I recommend *A Dictionary of Contemporary American Usage* by Bergen and Cornelia Evans and *A Concise Dictionary of Correct English* by B. A. Phythian.

adjective. A word that qualifies a noun or pronoun: 'a *brick* house', 'a *small* boy', 'a *blue* dress'. Most adjectives have three forms: the positive (*big*), the comparative (*bigger*) and the superlative (*biggest*). Although adjectives are usually easy to recognize when they stand before a noun, they are not always so easily discerned when they appear elsewhere in a sentence, as here: 'He was *deaf*', 'I'm glad to be *alive*', 'She's *awake* now'. Adjectives sometimes function as nouns (the *old*, the *poor*, the *sick*, the *insane*) and sometimes as adverbs (a *bitter*-cold night, a *quick*-witted man). The distinction between an adjective and an adverb is often very fine. In 'a great book', *great* is an adjective; but in 'a great many books', it is an adverb.

adverb. A word that qualifies (or describes) any word other than a noun. That may seem a loose definition, but, as Palmer says, the classification is 'quite clearly a "ragbag" or "dustbin", the category into which words that do not seem to belong elsewhere are placed'. In general, adverbs qualify verbs (*badly* played), adjectives (*too* loud) or other adverbs (*very* quickly). As with adjectives, they have the three forms of positive, comparative and superlative (seen respectively in *long, longer, longest*). A common misconception is the belief that words that end in *-ly* are always adverbs. *Kindly, sickly, masterly* and *deadly*, for example, are usually adjectives.

case. The term describes relationships or syntactic functions between parts of speech. A pronoun is in the nominative case (sometimes called the subjective) when it is the subject of a verb ('*He* is here') and in the accusative (sometimes called the objective) when it is the object of a verb or preposition ('Give it to *him*'). Except for six pairs of pronouns (*I/me, he/him, she/her, they/them, we/us* and *who/whom*) and the genitive (which see), English has shed all its case forms.

clause. A group of words that contains a true verb (i.e., a verb functioning as such) and subject. In the sentence 'The house, which was built in 1920, was white' there are two clauses: 'The house was white' and 'which was built in 1920'. The first, which would stand on its own, is called a main or principal or independent clause. The second, which would not stand on its own, is called a dependent or subordinate clause. Sometimes the subject is suppressed in main clauses, as here: 'He got up and went downstairs'. Although 'and went downstairs' would not stand on its own, it is a main clause because the subject has been suppressed. In effect the sentence is saying: 'He got up and he went downstairs'. (See also PHRASE.)

complement. A word or group of words that completes a predicate construction – that is, that provides full sense to the meaning of the verb. In 'He is a rascal', *rascal* is the complement of the verb *is*.

conjunction. A word that links grammatical equivalents, as in 'The President and Prime Minister conferred for two hours' (the conjunction *and* links two nouns) and 'He came yesterday, but he didn't stay long' (the conjunction *but* links two clauses).

genitive. A noun, pronoun or adjective is in the genitive case when it expresses possession (*my* house, *his* car, *John's* job). Although some authorities make very small distinctions between genitives and possessives, many others do not. In this book, I have used the term *possessives* throughout.

gerund. A verb made to function as a noun, as with the italicized words here: '*Seeing* is *believing*'; '*Cooking* is an art'; '*Walking* is good exercise'. Gerunds always end in *-ing*.

infinitive. The term describes verbs that are in the infinite mood (that is, that do not have a subject). Put another way, it is a verb form that indicates the action of the verb without inflection to indicate person, number or tense. There are two forms of infinitive: the full (*to go*, *to see*) and bare (*go*, *see*), often called simply 'an infinitive without *to*'.

mood. Verbs have four moods:
1. The indicative, which is used to state facts or ask questions (I *am* going; What time *is* it?);
2. The imperative, which indicates commands (*Come* here; *Leave* me alone);
3. The infinite, which makes general statements and has no subject (*To know* her is *to love* her);
4. The subjunctive, which is principally used to indicate hypotheses or suppositions (If I *were* you . . .). The uses of the subjunctive are discussed more fully in the body of the book.

noun is usually defined as a word that describes a person, place, thing or quality. Such a definition, as many authorities have noted, is technically inadequate. Most of us would not think of *hope*, *despair* and *exultation* as things, yet they are nouns. And most of the words that describe qualities – *good*, *bad*, *happy* and the like – are not nouns but adjectives. Palmer notes that there is no difference whatever in sense between 'He suffered terribly' and 'His suffering was terrible', yet *suffered* is a verb and *suffering* a noun.

There is, in short, no definition for *noun* that isn't circular, though happily for most of us it is one part of speech that is almost always instantly recognizable.

object. Whereas the subject of a sentence tells you who or what is performing an action, the object tells you on whom or on what the action is being performed. In 'I like you', *you* is the object of the verb *like*. In 'They have now built most of the house', *most of the house* is the object of the verb *built*. Sometimes sentences have direct and indirect objects, as here: 'Please send me four tickets'; 'I'll give the dog a bath' (cited by Phythian). The direct objects are *four tickets* and *a bath*. The indirect objects are *me* and *the dog*. Prepositions also have objects. In the sentence 'Give it to him', *him* is the object of the preposition *to*.

participle. The participle is a verbal adjective. There are two kinds: present participles, which end in *-ing* (*walking*, *looking*), and past participles, which end in *-d* (*heard*), *-ed* (*learned*), *-n* (*broken*) or *-t* (*bent*). The terms present and past participle can be misleading because present participles are often used in past-tense senses ('They were looking for the money') and past participles are often used when the sense is of the present or future ('He has broken it'; 'Things have never looked better'). When present-tense participles are used to function as nouns, they are called gerunds.

phrase. A group of words that does not have a subject and verb. 'I will come sometime soon' consists of a clause (*I will come*) and phrase (*sometime soon*). Phrases always express incomplete thoughts.

predicate. Everything in a sentence that is not part of the subject (i.e., the verb, its qualifiers and complements) is called the predicate. In 'The man went to town after work', *The man* is the subject and the rest of the sentence is the predicate. The verb alone is sometimes called the simple predicate.

preposition. A word that connects and specifies the relationship between a noun or noun equivalent and a verb, adjective or other noun or noun equivalent. In 'We climbed over the fence', the preposition *over* connects the verb *climbed* with the noun *fence*. Whether a word is a preposition or conjunction is often a matter of function. In 'The army attacked before the enemy was awake', *before* is a conjunction. But in 'The army attacked before dawn', *before* is a preposition. The distinction is that in the first sentence *before* is followed by a verb. In the second it is not.

pronoun. A word used in place of a noun or nouns. In 'I like walking and reading; such are my pleasures', *such* is a pronoun standing for *reading* and *walking*. Pronouns have been variously grouped by different authorities. Among the more common groupings are personal pronouns (*I, me, his,* etc.), relative pronouns (*who, whom, that, which*), demonstrative pronouns (*this, that, these, those*) and indefinite pronouns (*some, several, either, neither,* etc.).

subject. The word or phrase in a sentence or clause that indicates who or what is performing the action. In 'I see you', the subject is *I.* In 'Climbing steep hills tires me', *Climbing steep hills* is the subject.

substantive. A word or group of words that performs the function of a noun. In 'Swimming is good for you', *Swimming* is a substantive, as well as a gerund.

verb. Verbs can be defined generally (if a bit loosely) as words that have tense and that denote what someone or something is or does. Verbs that have an object are called transitive verbs – that is, the verb transmits the action from a subject to an object, as in 'He put the book on the table'. Verbs that do not have an object are called intransitive verbs, as in 'He slept all night'; in these the action is confined to the subject.

When it is necessary to indicate more than simple past or

present tense, two or more verbs are combined, as in 'I *have thought* about this all week'. Although there is no widely agreed term for such a combination of verbs, I have for convenience followed Fowler in this book and referred to them as compound verbs. The additional or 'helping' verb in such constructions (e.g., *have* in the example above) is called an auxiliary.